This Book Found You Because Your Soul whispered

A Compassionate Guide to Healing, Wholeness, and Coming Home to Yourself

The Soul's Experience

Beronica Parham

Table of Contents

DEDICATION

This book is dedicated to every soul who has ever felt lost,

who has searched for answers in all the wrong places, Who has forgotten their own light?

This book is your reminder. You were never broken. You are whole, you are enough, you are home.

INTRODUCTION

There is a reason this book found you.

Not by chance. Not by accident. It arrived because something deep within you whispered for more: more truth, more freedom, more alignment with who you really are.

Maybe you have felt it for years, a quiet ache beneath the surface of your life. A longing for something deeper than the roles you play and the masks you wear. Perhaps you have tried everything, read the books, attended the workshops, practiced the affirmations, yet still, something feels missing.

That missing piece is not outside of you. It never was. It is the part of you that has been waiting patiently for your return, the part that knows you are whole, even when you feel broken.

This book is not about fixing you. You are not broken. It is about remembering. Remembering what has always been true: you are worthy. You are enough. You are a divine expression of life itself.

This is not a quick fix. It is a sacred unfolding, a journey back to yourself. And by opening these pages, you have already said yes.

"What you seek is seeking you." — Rumi.

PREFACE
A Letter to You

To the ones who have felt the quiet ache beneath the noise of life…

To those who have carried invisible wounds, wondering if wholeness was ever meant for them…

To the seekers who have searched outside for answers, only to discover the longing was for their own truth…

To the brave hearts repeating patterns they no longer wish to live, sensing there is more, yet unsure how to reach it…

This book is for you.

Within these pages, may you find not just words, but mirrors, reflections of the light you thought you had lost. May you remember that your essence has never been broken, only hidden beneath layers of forgetting.

You are not here to fix yourself. You are here to awaken to what has always been: your worth, your voice, your infinite capacity to love and be loved.

You are a sacred expression of life itself. You are whole. You are enough. You are home.

Let these words guide you back, not to something new, but to the truth that has been waiting within you all along.

PART ONE
Awakening to Your Truth

CHAPTER 1
The Whisper That Led You Here The Call Beneath the Noise

Life is loud. It fills our days with obligations, expectations, and endless distractions. Notifications ping, calendars overflow, and the world constantly demands more productivity, more achievement, more proof that you are "enough."

In that noise, the voice of your soul can feel faint, almost imperceptible. But it never stops speaking. It calls you in moments of stillness, when you pause long enough to feel the ache in your chest, the heaviness in your heart, the question that will not go away:

Is this all there is?

That question is not despair. It is an invitation, an invitation to remember who you are beyond the roles you play and the masks you wear.

The whisper often comes when you least expect it, while driving alone, staring at the ceiling at night, or watching rain slide down a windowpane. It does not shout. It does not demand. It simply waits for you to notice.

And when you do, something shifts. You realize that the life you have been living may look "fine" on the outside, but inside, your soul is longing for depth, truth, and freedom. The call beneath the noise is not asking you to abandon everything. It is asking you to come home to yourself.

The whisper comes when you have outgrown the life you have been living. It arrives when your soul is ready for more authenticity, more alignment, more meaning. You feel it because you are awakening.

Awakening is not a single moment; it is a series of gentle nudges that remind you:

You are not here to merely survive.

You are not here to live by someone else's script.

You are here to embody your truth and express your light.

The whisper often begins as discomfort, a sense that something is missing, even when everything looks "right." That discomfort is not failure; it is guidance. It is your soul saying: "There is more for you. There is a deeper way to live."

You feel the whisper because you are ready, ready to peel back the layers of conditioning, fear, and self-doubt. Ready to remember what has always been true: You are whole. You are worthy. You are a divine expression of life itself.

The whisper is not a demand; it is an invitation. And by opening this book, you have already said yes.

Reflection: A Moment of Truth

I remember sitting in a crowded coffee shop one afternoon, surrounded by laughter and conversation, yet feeling utterly alone. My life looked "successful" on the outside: career milestones, social connections, a calendar full of plans. But inside, something was missing. It was not sadness exactly; it was a quiet ache, a longing for something deeper.

As I stared out the window, watching raindrops race down the glass, a thought whispered through me: "This is not who I am." It was not loud. It was not dramatic. But it was undeniable. That whisper became the turning point, the moment I realized that no external achievement could fill the emptiness of living disconnected from my soul.

Maybe you have had a similar moment. Perhaps that is why you are here. If so, know this: that whisper is not a flaw. It is an invitation.

Wisdom to Carry Forward

"The wound is the place where the Light enters you." (*Rumi*)

"The privilege of a lifetime is to become who you truly are." (*Carl Jung*)

"What you seek is seeking you." (*Rumi*)

Affirmation

I trust the voice within.

My soul knows the way.

I am safe to listen to my inner truth.

Every whisper leads me closer to myself.

Journal Prompts

- Take time to reflect on these questions:
- When was the last time I felt deeply connected to myself?
- What patterns or roles feel heavy or outdated in my life?
- If my soul could speak freely, what would it say to me today?
- What does "wholeness" mean to me?

Soul Practice: The Whisper Practice

Find a quiet space where you will not be disturbed. Close your eyes and place your hand on your heart.

Take three slow, deep breaths, feeling your chest rise and fall.

Ask yourself gently: "What is my soul whispering right now?"

Write down the first words, feelings, or images that arise, without judgment, without editing. Trust what comes. This is your soul speaking.

Guided Meditation: Listening to the Whisper

Sit comfortably and close your eyes. Take three deep breaths, letting your body soften with each exhale.

Imagine yourself in a serene forest. The air is fresh, and the sound of leaves rustling soothes you. Ahead, there is a quiet clearing bathed in golden light. Walk toward it slowly.

In the center of the clearing is a small flame, a symbol of your soul's voice. Sit beside the flame and ask: "What do you want me to know?"

Listen. Do not force. Just receive. When ready, thank the flame and return to the present moment.

Write down what you heard or felt.

Insight to Carry Forward

The whisper you heard is not random. It is the beginning of your return to yourself. Every time you pause and listen, you strengthen the bridge back to your own truth. This chapter is your doorway. The next chapter will guide you through it by uncovering the patterns that keep you stuck and how to release them gently.

CHAPTER 2
Breaking the Patterns That Keep You Stuck

Patterns are the invisible threads that weave through our lives, connecting past to present, reaction to reaction. They feel familiar because they are; they have been with us so long that we mistake them for identity. But patterns are not who you are. They are simply what you learned to do to survive.

The Weight of Repetition

There is a heaviness that comes from living the same story over and over. You wake up with good intentions, promising yourself that this time will be different. But then, almost without thinking, you find yourself back in the same cycle, reacting the same way, choosing the same kind of relationships, falling into the same habits.

It feels frustrating. It feels defeating. And if you are like most people, you have probably asked yourself: "What is wrong with me? Why can't I change?"

Here is the truth: Nothing is wrong with you. Repeating patterns do not mean you are broken; they mean you are human. It means your nervous system is doing what it was designed to do: keep you safe, even if that safety comes at the cost of your joy.

The weight of repetition is not just about the choices you make; it is about the beliefs beneath those choices. Beliefs like: "I am only lovable if I please everyone," "Conflict means abandonment," and "If I fail, I am worthless."

These beliefs were formed long ago, often in moments when you needed protection. They became the blueprint for how you navigate life. And until you rewrite that blueprint, the same story will keep playing.

But here is the good news: You can rewrite it. You can choose differently. And every new choice is a step toward freedom.

Why Patterns Exist

Patterns are not random. They are survival strategies. When you were younger, maybe as a child, maybe as a teenager, you learned what kept you safe, loved, and accepted. You learned what helped you avoid pain. And you adapted.

If love felt conditional, you learned to perform. If conflict felt dangerous, you learned to stay silent. If rejection felt unbearable, you learned to cling or withdraw.

These patterns were brilliant solutions at the time. They helped you cope in environments where you lacked control. They were your armor. But now, as an adult, that armor has become heavy. It limits your movement. It keeps you from breathing freely.

Understanding this is powerful because it shifts the narrative from "I am failing" to "I am protecting myself." And when you see your patterns through the lens of compassion, you stop fighting yourself and start healing yourself.

The Compassionate Truth

Before you rush to "fix" yourself, pause. You do not need fixing. You need understanding. You need gentleness. You need to meet yourself where you are, with love, not judgment.

Your patterns are not enemies. They are teachers. They reveal where you have been wounded and where you long to heal. They show you the places that still ache for safety, for belonging, for love.

When you approach your patterns with curiosity instead of criticism, something shifts. You stop asking, "What is wrong with me?" and start asking, "What happened to me?"

That question opens the door to compassion. And compassion opens the door to change. Here is the truth: You cannot shame yourself into transformation, but you can love yourself into freedom.

Reflection: A Moment of Truth

I once knew someone who had spent years saying "yes" to everything: every request, every demand, every invitation. On the surface, they seemed generous and dependable. But inside, they were exhausted, resentful, and quietly angry.

When we explored this pattern together, they realized it began in childhood. Saying "yes" was how they earned love and avoided rejection. It was a survival strategy. But now, as an adult, it was draining their energy and eroding their sense of self.

The breakthrough came when they understood this: "I am not broken. I am just living by an old rule that no longer serves me."

That awareness was the first step toward change. And that is where your journey begins, too.

Wisdom to Carry Forward

"Until you make the unconscious conscious, it will direct your life, and you will call it fate." (**Carl Jung**)

"You are allowed to outgrow people, places, and patterns that no longer fit the person you are becoming." (**Unknown**)

"Freedom is not the absence of something. It is the presence of your true self." (**Unknown**)

I am free to choose differently. I release what no longer serves me and embrace what honors my truth.

Journal Prompts

Reflect deeply on these questions:

- What patterns keep showing up in my life? (Think relationships, habits, thoughts.)
- When did I first learn this pattern? What was it protecting me from?
- What does this pattern cost me now—emotionally, mentally, spiritually?
- If I were free from this pattern, how would my life feel?
- What new belief would support the change I desire?

Soul Practice

Pattern Mapping Exercise:

1. **Identify the Pattern:** Write down one recurring pattern that feels heavy or limiting.

2. **Trace Its Roots:** Ask yourself, "When did I first notice this behavior? What was happening in my life?"

3. **Name the Need:** What need was this pattern trying to meet? (Safety? Love? Approval?)

4. **Create a New Choice:** Write one empowering alternative you can choose next time. Example: Old Pattern: saying "yes" to everything to avoid rejection. New Choice: "I honor my limits and say no with love."

5. **Anchor It:** Write your new choice on a note and place it somewhere visible. Repeat it daily until it feels natural.

Guided Meditation

Close your eyes and take three deep breaths.

Imagine yourself standing in a dimly lit room. This room represents your old patterns. Look around. Notice the walls and the objects-symbols of habits that no longer serve you.

In front of you is a door. Beyond it is light, freedom, and possibility.

Walk toward the door. Place your hand on the handle. Whisper: "I choose freedom."

Open the door and step into the light. Feel the warmth on your skin. Breathe deeply.

Repeat silently: "I am free to choose differently."

When ready, return to the present moment and write down what you felt.

Insight to Carry Forward

Breaking patterns is not about force; it is about awareness and choice. Every time you choose differently, you rewrite your story. You reclaim your power. The next chapter will guide you into the heart of your emotions, the messengers that hold the keys to your healing.

CHAPTER 3
Meeting Your Emotions with Compassion

Emotions are not flaws in your design; they are part of your brilliance. They are signals, guiding you toward what matters most. Yet, for many of us, emotions have been misunderstood. We were taught to fear them, to hide them, to treat them as weaknesses. But emotions are not here to control you; they are here to inform you.

The Truth About Emotions

- **Fear says:** "Pay attention. Something needs care."
- **Anger says:** "A boundary has been crossed."
- **Sadness says:** "It is time to let go."

- **Joy says:** "You are aligned with your truth."

When you silence these signals, you disconnect from your inner compass. You lose the wisdom that emotions carry. The truth is, emotions are energy in motion; they are meant to move through you, not stay trapped inside. When you allow them to flow, they become bridges to healing and clarity.

Why We Resist Feeling

We resist emotions because we have been conditioned to believe they are dangerous. Somewhere along the way, we learned that crying makes us weak, that anger makes us bad, that vulnerability makes us unsafe. So, we built walls. We armored up.

But here is what happens when we resist: The sadness we avoid turns into numbness. The anger we suppress turns into resentment. The fear we deny turns into anxiety.

Resistance does not erase emotions; it amplifies them. What we push away does not disappear; it waits. And the longer we wait, the heavier it becomes.

The truth? Feeling is not the same as drowning. You can feel deeply and remain whole. You can allow emotions without being consumed by them. In fact, when you do, you reclaim your power.

The Compassionate Approach

Compassion is the antidote to resistance. It is the voice that says, "It is okay to feel this. I am safe to feel this."

When you meet your emotions with compassion, you stop fighting yourself. You stop labeling feelings as "good" or "bad" and start seeing them as messengers. You create space for them to speak, and in that space, healing begins.

Compassion means slowing down. It means breathing through discomfort. It means reminding yourself: I am not my emotions; I am the one who holds them. I can feel this and still be safe.

This is not a weakness; it is a strength. True strength is not about suppressing what you feel; it is about embracing it with grace.

Reflection: A Moment of Truth

I once worked with a client who had spent years avoiding grief after losing a loved one. They stayed busy, smiled through the pain, and told themselves they were "fine." But inside, the weight grew heavier. It showed up as anxiety, exhaustion, and even physical illness.

When they finally allowed themselves to cry, really cry, the release was profound. It was not weakness; it was liberation. They said, "I thought feeling this would break me. Instead, it set me free."

Your emotions are not here to break you. They are here to heal you.

Wisdom to Carry Forward

"Feelings are just visitors; let them come and go." (*Rumi*)

"What we resist persists." (*Carl Jung*)

"You do not have to control your thoughts. You just have to stop letting them control you." (*Dan Millman*)

Affirmation

My emotions are sacred messengers. I allow myself to feel without judgment. Every emotion I experience is valid and safe.

Journal Prompts

Reflect deeply on these questions:

- Which emotion do I resist most? Why?
- What story do I tell myself about feeling this emotion?
- How would it feel to welcome this emotion instead of fighting it?
- What emotion feels easiest for me to express? What does that reveal?

Soul Practice

Emotional Check-In Practice:

Set a timer for three minutes. Close your eyes and ask: "What am I feeling right now?"

Name the emotion without labeling it "good" or "bad." Place your hand on your heart and say: "It is okay to feel this."

Repeat this practice daily to build emotional awareness and a sense of safety.

Guided Meditation

Sit comfortably and close your eyes. Take three deep breaths, letting your body soften.

Imagine a warm, safe space, a room filled with soft light. In this space, every emotion is welcome.

Now, picture one emotion you have been avoiding. See it as a gentle presence entering the room.

Ask it: "What do you want me to know?" Listen without judgment.

When you are ready, thank the emotion and let it dissolve into light.

Open your eyes and write down what you heard.

Insight to Carry Forward

Your emotions are not obstacles; they are bridges. Every time you honor what you feel, you move closer to your authentic self. The next chapter will help you fully reclaim your authentic self by removing the masks and living in alignment with your truth.

CHAPTER 4
Reclaiming Your Authentic Self The Masks We Wear

From the moment we enter this world, we begin learning what is acceptable, what earns love, what avoids rejection, and what keeps us safe. Slowly, quietly, we start wearing masks. We smile when we want to cry. We say "yes" when our soul screams "no." We shrink ourselves to fit spaces that were never meant for us.

These masks are not lies; they are survival strategies. They helped you navigate environments where being fully yourself did not feel safe. But now, those masks have become heavy. They block your light. They silence your truth. They keep you from living the life your soul longs for.

Every mask you wear has a story:

- The mask of pleasing says, "If I make everyone happy, I will be loved."
- The mask of achievement says, "If I succeed, I will be enough."
- The mask of strength says, "If I never show weakness, I will be safe."

But here is the truth: masks may protect you, but they also disconnect you from yourself and from others. Real connection only happens when you show up as you truly are.

The question is not whether you wear masks. We all do. The question is: Are you ready to take them off?

Why We Hide

We hide because we fear that if people see the real us, the messy, imperfect, vulnerable us, they will turn away. We fear rejection. We fear judgment. We fear abandonment. So, we trade authenticity for approval.

But approval is fleeting. Authenticity is freedom.

When you live behind a mask, you may feel accepted, but you will never feel truly seen. And being seen fully, deeply, unapologetically is what your soul craves.

The cost of hiding is high. You lose your voice. You lose your joy. You lose the chance to live a life that feels like yours. The relationships you build are with your persona, not your person. The love you receive feels conditional because it is based on who you pretend to be, not who you are.

Hiding feels safer than being seen. But safety without authenticity is a prison. Sooner or later, every soul grows tired of captivity.

The truth? You are not here to be perfect. You are here to be real.

Imperfection is not your flaw; it is your humanity.

Vulnerability is not your weakness; it is your bridge to connection. And the parts of you that you have hidden for so long? They are not shameful. They are sacred.

The Courage to Be Seen

Reclaiming your authentic self is not about becoming someone new. It is about remembering who you were before the world told you who to be. It is about peeling back the layers of conditioning and rediscovering the essence that has always been there.

Authenticity is not perfection. It is truth. It is saying: "This is who I am. This is what I feel. This is what I need." And trusting that you are worthy of love, not for the mask you wear, but for the soul you are.

Courage does not mean you will not feel fear. It means you choose truth even when fear whispers, "Hide." It means you risk being seen because the cost of hiding has become too great.

When you choose authenticity, some people may not understand. Some may even walk away. And that is okay. The people who are meant for you will love you not despite your truth, but because of it.

Being authentic means showing up as you are on good days and hard days, in strength and in struggle, in light and in shadow. It means permitting yourself to be human. To make mistakes. To change your mind. To grow.

It means releasing the exhausting performance of perfection and embracing the liberating practice of presence.

The world does not need another perfect person. It needs you to be real, raw, and radiant in your truth.

Reflection: A Moment of Truth

I remember a dear friend who seemed to have everything together: a successful career, a beautiful home and a curated social media presence. But one evening over coffee, they confessed something that broke my heart:

"I feel like I am living someone else's life. Every decision I make is about what people expect, not what I want. I do not even know who I am anymore."

They had spent years performing, saying "yes" when they wanted to say "no," smiling when they wanted to cry, chasing achievements for validation rather than joy. When they began removing the masks, speaking their truth, setting boundaries, and saying "no" without guilt, they felt terrified at first.

But then something miraculous happened: they felt alive.

"For the first time," they said, "I feel like I am breathing my own air."

That is the power of authenticity. It is not easy, but it is liberating. It is not comfortable, but it is real. And real is what your soul has been longing for all along.

Wisdom to Carry Forward

"Owning our story and loving ourselves through that process is the bravest thing we will ever do." (**Brené Brown,** *The Gifts of Imperfection)*

"To be yourself in a world that is constantly trying to make you something else is the greatest accomplishment." (**Ralph Waldo Emerson,** *Self-Reliance)*

"Authenticity is the daily practice of letting go of who we think we are supposed to be and embracing who we are." (**Brené Brown,** *The Gifts of Imperfection)*

Affirmation

I am safe to be seen. I am free to be me. I choose authenticity over approval.

Journal Prompts

Take time to reflect deeply on these questions:

- Where in my life do I feel most authentic?
- Where do I feel like I am performing?
- What would change if I showed up as my true self?
- What mask am I most afraid to remove? What would happen if I did?
- Who in my life knows the real me? How does that feel?

Soul Practice

The Mask Release Ritual

This exercise helps you identify and release the roles and masks that no longer serve you.

1. Take a sheet of paper and write down the masks you wear. Examples: "The Pleaser," "The Achiever," "The Strong One," "The Perfect Parent," "The Caretaker."
2. For each mask, write:
3. Why did I start wearing this mask?
4. What has it protected me from?
5. What does it cost me now?
6. When you are ready, tear or burn the paper (safely) as a symbolic act of release.
7. Whisper or speak aloud: "I am free to be my authentic self."

8. In the days following this ritual, notice when you feel the urge to put the mask back on. Pause. Breathe. Choose differently.

Guided Meditation

Sit comfortably and close your eyes. Take three deep breaths, letting your body soften with each exhale.

Imagine yourself standing in a beautiful open field. The sun is warm, and the air feels pure. You are safe here. You are free here.

Ahead of you is a version of yourself, radiant, confident, and authentic. They are smiling at you. This is you without masks, without pretense, without fear.

Walk toward them slowly. Notice what they are wearing, how they stand, and the energy they radiate. There is a lightness about them, A peace.

When you reach them, they embrace you. You feel their warmth, their acceptance, their love.

Ask them: "What truth do you want me to live today?"

Listen. Receive the message. It may come as words, feelings, images, or simply a knowing.

Place your hand on your heart and repeat: "I am safe to be seen. I am free to be me."

When ready, open your eyes and write down what you heard or felt.

Insight to Carry Forward

Authenticity is not about being liked by everyone. It is about loving yourself. Every time you choose truth over performance, you reclaim a piece of your soul. The next chapter will guide you toward healing the wounded child within the part of you that first learned to hide.

CHAPTER 5
Healing the Inner Child The Child Within

Inside every adult lives a child, a tender, innocent part of you that once believed in magic, love, and safety. This child laughed freely, cried openly, and trusted without fear. But somewhere along the way, life happened. Words were spoken that wounded. Needs went unmet. Love felt conditional. And so, that child learned to adapt.

- They learned to hide their feelings.
- They learned to be "good" to earn approval.
- They learned that vulnerability was dangerous.

Those lessons became patterns. Those patterns became armor. And now, as an adult, you may still be carrying the weight of that child's pain.

Healing the inner child is not about dwelling in the past; it is about giving yourself what you needed then, now. It is about becoming the safe place you have always longed for.

Your inner child does not need you to be perfect. They need you to be present. They need you to see them, hear them, and love them unconditionally. Because that is what every child deserves, and that is what you deserved then and deserve now.

Why Inner Child Healing Matters

When the child within you feels unseen, unheard, or unloved, they speak through your present life. They speak through fear of abandonment in relationships, through perfectionism that whispers, "If I am perfect, I will be loved," through anger or anxiety that erupts when old wounds are triggered.

These reactions are not flaws; they are echoes, echoes of a time when you did not have the tools to cope. But now, you do.

Healing your inner child allows you to break cycles, reclaim joy, and live from a place of wholeness rather than woundedness. When you nurture this child, you soften the grip of old patterns. You stop seeking love in places that cannot give it. You stop abandoning yourself to keep others close.

You begin to live from a truth that says: "I am worthy of love simply because I exist."

Inner child work is not regression; it is integration. It is gathering the scattered pieces of your soul and bringing them home. It is saying to every version of you that ever felt small, scared, or unworthy: "I see you now. You matter. You are safe with me."

This is how healing happens, not by erasing the past, but by rewriting the story you tell yourself about it.

The Compassionate Truth

Your inner child does not need judgment. They need love. They need someone to say: "I see you. I hear you. You matter." And that someone is you.

Healing is not about erasing the past; it is about rewriting the story you tell yourself about it. It is about replacing shame with compassion, fear with safety, and silence with voice.

Every time you choose to comfort that child within, you reclaim a piece of yourself that was lost. You become the parent, the protector, the nurturer you always needed. And in doing so, you set yourself free.

This does not mean the pain never happened. It means the pain no longer defines you. It means you can hold your younger self with tenderness and say: "You did the best you could. And now, I am here to take care of you."

When you heal your inner child, you heal your present self. You stop reacting to old wounds and start responding from wisdom. You stop seeking approval and start trusting your worth. You stop performing for love and start receiving it from yourself, first and foremost.

This is the most important relationship you will ever heal.

Reflection: A Moment of Truth

I remember working with a client who always seemed strong, always in control, always taking care of everyone else. But one day, they shared something that changed everything:

"I cannot remember the last time I felt safe just being me."

As we talked, they realized that as a child, they were praised for being "responsible" and "mature." They learned early that their worth came from taking care of others, not expressing their own needs. So, they buried their feelings and wore strength like armor.

When they began inner child work, writing letters to their younger self, speaking words of love they never heard, they cried for the first time in years, not tears of weakness, but tears of release.

They said, "I feel like I have finally come home to myself."

That is what healing does. It brings you home—not to a place, but to yourself.

Wisdom to Carry Forward

"It is never too late to have a happy childhood." **Tom Robbins,** *Still Life with Woodpecker*

"The child within us never dies; it waits for us to return and listen." (*Anonymous*)

"Healing does not mean the damage never existed. It means the damage no longer controls our lives." (*Akshay Dubey*)

Affirmation

I give myself the love I needed then. I am safe now. My feelings are valid. I am worthy of unconditional love.

Journal Prompts

Take time to reflect deeply on these questions:

- What did I need most as a child that I did not receive?
- What messages about love and worth did I learn growing up?
- How do those messages still affect me today?
- What would I say to my younger self right now?

- How can I give my inner child what they need today?

Soul Practice: Inner Child Letter

This practice helps you connect with and nurture your younger self.

1. Find a quiet space and a piece of paper. Close your eyes and picture yourself as a child, any age that feels significant.
2. Write a letter to your younger self. Begin with: "Dear [Your Name], I am so sorry you felt..."
3. Tell them what you wish someone had told you then:

   - "You are loved."
   - "You are enough."
   - "You are safe."
   - "What happened was not your fault."
   - "You did the best you could."

1. Read the letter aloud to yourself. Let the words sink in. Feel them in your body.
2. Place the letter somewhere special, or carry it with you as a reminder that you are now the safe space you always needed.

Guided Meditation

Sit comfortably and close your eyes. Take three deep breaths, feeling your body relax.

Imagine walking into a warm, safe room. In the center of the room is your younger self, maybe five, maybe ten years old. See them clearly. Notice what they are wearing, how they look.

Kneel beside them and say: "I am here now. I see you. I love you."

They may be scared. They may be sad. They may not trust you at first. That is okay. Stay present. Stay gentle.

Hold them in your arms if they let you. Feel their small body against yours. Let them know: "You are safe. You are enough. You are loved."

Whisper: "I will never leave you again. I am here to take care of you now."

Stay with them as long as you need. When you are ready, bring them back with you into your heart. Know that they are always with you now, safe and loved.

Open your eyes and place your hand on your heart. Breathe.

Insight to Carry Forward

Healing your inner child is not a one-time event; it is an ongoing practice of love, compassion, and presence. Every time you choose to honor your feelings, set boundaries, or speak your truth, you are reparenting yourself. You are giving that child what they always deserved. The next section will guide you through releasing resentment and reclaiming peace through forgiveness.

PART TWO
Releasing What No Longer Serves

CHAPTER 6
Forgiveness as Freedom The Weight of Unforgiveness

Unforgiveness is heavy. It sits in your chest like a stone, pressing against your breath and dimming your light. It shows up in sleepless nights, in the tension that knots your shoulders, and in the bitterness that colors your words.

When you refuse to forgive, you carry the offender with you everywhere, into your thoughts, your dreams, and your future. You replay the hurt like a broken record, reopening the wound each time. And while you may believe that holding on protects you, it actually imprisons you.

Think of it this way: every time you replay the hurt, you reopen the wound. You give the past permission to invade your present. The person who hurt you may have moved on, but you remain shackled to yesterday.

The weight of unforgiveness is not just emotional; it is spiritual and physical as well. Studies show that chronic resentment raises cortisol levels, weakens the immune system, and increases the risk of heart disease. Beyond the science, there is something deeper: unforgiveness blocks the flow of love and peace that your soul longs for.

Holding onto anger is like drinking poison and expecting the other person to die. The only person suffering is you.

Why Forgiveness Matters

Forgiveness is not just a moral ideal; it is a lifeline for your emotional and spiritual well-being. When you forgive, you reclaim the energy that resentment has been draining from your soul.

Every grudge you hold is like a thread tying you to the past and keeping you from fully stepping into the present. Forgiveness matters because it restores your power. It says, "I will not let what hurt me define me."

Forgiveness is not about condoning harm or forgetting pain. It is not about letting someone off the hook or pretending the hurt never happened. Forgiveness is about liberating yourself from the chains of resentment.

It is choosing peace over pain and freedom over fear. It is the moment you decide that your joy is worth more than your anger.

Science supports this truth. Research shows that forgiveness lowers stress hormones, improves heart health, and enhances mental clarity. Beyond the science, forgiveness is a sacred act of liberation. It is choosing to break free from the prison of the past.

When you forgive, you are not saying what happened was okay. You are saying, "I refuse to let this continue to hurt me."

The Freedom of Letting Go

Letting go is not about erasing the memory or excusing the harm; it is about releasing the grip that pain has on your life. Forgiveness is a gift you give yourself. It is the moment you say, "I choose to be free."

When you forgive, you open the door to healing. You create space for joy to return, for hope to bloom, and for love to flow again. Freedom feels like breathing deeply after years of shallow breaths. It feels like sunlight breaking through clouds that have lingered too long.

Forgiveness does not change the past, but it transforms your future. It is an act of courage and compassion, and it begins with a single choice: to let go.

Some forgiveness is immediate, a sudden release, a weight lifted. Other forgiveness is gradual, a daily practice of choosing freedom over bitterness and peace over anger. Both are valid. Both are powerful.

Remember, forgiveness is not for them. It is for you. It is your declaration of independence from pain, your reclaiming of the life that resentment has stolen.

You deserve to be free. And forgiveness is the key.

Reflection: A Moment of Truth

I once held onto anger like a badge of honor. Someone I loved deeply betrayed my trust, and I vowed never to forgive. Years passed, and the bitterness became my shadow, following me everywhere.

One day, I realized something profound: the person who hurt me had moved on, living unburdened, while I was still chained to yesterday. They were not thinking about me, but I was thinking about them constantly. They were free, and I was imprisoned.

That day, I whispered, "I forgive you." It was not instant magic. The anger did not disappear immediately, but it was the first crack in the wall I had built around my heart.

Forgiveness did not change what happened, but it changed me. It freed me. Slowly, the stone in my chest began to dissolve. I could breathe again. I could hope again. I could love again.

Forgiveness was not weakness; it was the strongest thing I ever did.

Wisdom to Carry Forward

"Forgiveness is the fragrance that the violet sheds on the heel that has crushed it." (*Mark Twain*)

"Holding onto anger is like grasping a hot coal with the intent of throwing it at someone else; you are the one who gets burned." (*Buddha*)

"Forgiveness is not an occasional act; it is a constant attitude." (*Martin Luther King Jr.*)

Affirmation

I release the weight of resentment. I choose peace over pain. Forgiveness sets me free.

Journal Prompts

Take time to reflect deeply on these questions:

- Who am I still holding resentment toward, and why?
- What would my life feel like if I let this go?
- What lessons did this experience teach me about myself?
- How can I honor my boundaries while practicing forgiveness?
- What am I afraid will happen if I forgive?

Soul Practice

The Stone Release Ritual

This practice helps you physically and symbolically release the burden of unforgiveness.

1. Find a small stone, one that fits comfortably in your hand. Hold it and imagine it represents the hurt, anger, or resentment you have been carrying.
2. Sit quietly with the stone. Feel its weight. Notice how heavy it feels to hold onto this pain.
3. Speak aloud or silently what this stone represents: "This stone is the anger I feel toward [person or situation]. This stone is the hurt that I have carried for [length of time]."
4. When you are ready, say: "I release this pain. I reclaim my peace. I choose freedom."
5. Place the stone in flowing water, such as a river, stream, or ocean, or bury it in the earth as a symbol

41

of letting go. As you release the stone, visualize the burden lifting from your shoulders.

6. Walk away without looking back. Notice how your body feels lighter and freer.

Guided Meditation

Close your eyes. Breathe deeply. Picture yourself standing in a serene meadow. In your hands, you hold a heavy rope tied to a dark cloud above you. This cloud represents the pain, anger, or resentment you have been holding.

Feel the weight of the rope in your hands. Notice how tiring it is to hold on.

With each exhale, loosen your grip slightly. Feel the tension in your hands dissolving. Feel the cloud beginning to drift.

Say to yourself: "I forgive, not because you deserve it, but because I deserve peace."

When you are ready, release the rope completely. Watch as the cloud drifts away into the horizon, becoming smaller and smaller until it disappears.

Feel the lightness in your chest. Feel the space where the burden used to be. Breathe into that space.

Whisper softly: "I am free."

Open your eyes when you are ready.

Insight to Carry Forward

Forgiveness is not a one-time act; it is a daily choice. Each time resentment knocks, choose freedom. Each time anger whispers, choose peace. You are not defined by what hurt you; you are defined by how you heal. The next chapter invites you to explore the courage of vulnerability, the strength found in softness.

CHAPTER 7
Embracing Vulnerability Why Vulnerability Matters

Vulnerability is often misunderstood as weakness, yet it is the birthplace of connection, creativity, and courage. To be vulnerable is to stand in your truth without armor, to let others see the raw, unpolished parts of your soul. It is the quiet strength that whispers, "I am enough, even when I am imperfect."

When we hide behind walls, we trade authenticity for acceptance. But true belonging only happens when we show up as we are, flawed, tender, and real. Vulnerability is not about oversharing; it is about opening the door to intimacy and trust. It is the soil where love grows and the light that dissolves shame.

Vulnerability matters because it is the heartbeat of authentic living. Without it, we live behind walls, safe but disconnected. Research confirms what the heart already knows: vulnerability deepens relationships, strengthens resilience, and fuels innovation.

When you allow yourself to be vulnerable, you invite intimacy, trust, and genuine connection. It is saying, "This is me, unmasked, imperfect, and real," and trusting that you are worthy of love not for your perfection, but for your essence.

Vulnerability dismantles the illusion of perfection and reminds us that we are human, not machines, not flawless beings, but souls craving connection. Without it, we live in isolation, performing for approval instead of living in truth.

The Fear of Being Seen

We fear vulnerability because we fear rejection. We worry that if people see our cracks, they will turn away. So, we build walls, walls of humor, achievement, and silence. We curate our lives like museum exhibits, showing only what shines and hiding what hurts.

But those walls keep out love as much as they keep out judgment. They protect us from pain, yes, but they also protect us from joy. The truth is, vulnerability does not guarantee acceptance, but it guarantees freedom. It frees you from the exhausting performance of perfection.

The fear of being seen is rooted in shame, the belief that if someone knew the real you, they would not stay. But here is the paradox: the more you hide, the lonelier you become. The antidote to shame is courage, the courage to say, "Here I am, and I am enough."

When you risk being seen, something miraculous happens. The people who matter do not turn away; they come closer. They recognize their own humanity reflected in yours. And those who do turn away were never your people to begin with.

Being vulnerable does not mean you will never be hurt. It means you choose connection even when fear whispers that hiding is safer. It means you trust that your truth is more valuable than any mask you could wear.

The Strength in Softness

Softness is not weakness; it is power in its purest form. In a world that glorifies hardness and hustle, choosing vulnerability is revolutionary. It takes strength to admit you need help, to say you are hurting, to open your heart knowing it might break.

When you embrace vulnerability, you step into a strength that is rooted in authenticity. You stop hiding and start living. You discover that your imperfections are not liabilities; they are bridges to a deeper connection.

Vulnerability transforms fear into courage and shame into self-compassion. True strength is not in the armor; it is in the openness. It is in the willingness to love without guarantees, to speak truth without certainty, to show up fully human.

Softness is where resilience is born, because only when we bend can we avoid breaking. The willow survives the storm not because it is hard, but because it is flexible. And so, it is with us.

When you allow yourself to be vulnerable, you permit others to do the same. You create spaces where authenticity is valued over perfection, where connection matters more than image, and where love can flourish because it is rooted in truth.

This is the strength that changes everything. Not the strength to never fall, but the strength to rise and say, "I fell, and I am still worthy of love."

Reflection: A Moment of Truth

I used to believe that strength meant silence. I wore my independence like armor, never asking for help, never admitting pain. But inside, I was lonely. The walls I built to protect me also imprisoned me.

One day, exhausted from carrying everything alone, I told a friend, "I am struggling." I expected judgment, but instead, I found understanding. That moment changed me.

My friend said, "Thank you for trusting me with your truth. That took real courage." I realized then that vulnerability was not making me weaker; it was making me human. And in that humanity, I found strength I never knew I had.

The walls began to come down, not all at once, but slowly. And as they fell, love rushed in, not because I was perfect, but because I was real. That is the gift of vulnerability. It does not promise you will never be hurt. It promises you will be free.

Wisdom to Carry Forward

"Vulnerability is the birthplace of innovation, creativity, and change." (*Brené Brown*)

"The strongest love is the love that can demonstrate its fragility." (*Paulo Coelho*)

"Owning our story and loving ourselves through that process is the bravest thing we will ever do." (*Brené Brown*)

Affirmation

I honor my truth. I embrace my softness. Vulnerability is my strength.

Journal Prompts

Take time to reflect deeply on these questions:

- Where in my life am I hiding behind walls?
- What would it feel like to share my truth with someone I trust?
- What fears arise when I think about being vulnerable?
- How can I practice vulnerability without betraying myself?
- Who in my life has earned the right to see my tender places?

Soul Practice

The Mirror Truth Practice

This exercise helps you practice being seen, starting with yourself.

1. Stand before a mirror when you have privacy and quiet. Look into your own eyes.
2. Say aloud: "I see you. I accept you. You are enough."
3. Notice any resistance. Notice any emotions that arise. Tears are welcome here. Discomfort is normal.
4. Continue: "I am allowed to be imperfect. I am allowed to need help. I am allowed to be human."
5. Place your hand on your heart and breathe. Feel your own presence.

6. Repeat this practice daily. Over time, speaking your truth out loud will feel less foreign and more like coming home.

Guided Meditation

Close your eyes. Take three deep breaths. Feel your body settle.

Imagine yourself standing in a safe, warm space. You are holding a heavy cloak, the cloak of perfection, pretense, and protective armor.

Feel its weight on your shoulders. Notice how tiring it is to carry.

Slowly, you remove the cloak and place it on the ground. As it falls, you feel lighter, freer, more yourself.

A gentle light surrounds you, warm and accepting. This light does not judge. It simply sees you, all of you, and loves what it sees.

Whisper to yourself: "I am loved as I am. My vulnerability is sacred. I am safe to be seen."

Stay here, breathing in acceptance and breathing out fear. Let this image anchor in your heart.

When ready, open your eyes. Remember: you are worthy without the armor.

Insight to Carry Forward

Vulnerability is not a risk; it is a gift. It opens doors to love, trust, and growth. Each time you choose to be real, you choose freedom. You choose life. The next chapter invites you to anchor yourself in the present moment, where peace always resides.

CHAPTER 8
The Power of Presence Why Presence Matters

Presence is the art of being fully here, mind, body, and soul. In a world that glorifies speed and multitasking, presence feels like rebellion. It is choosing to pause when everything screams "hurry." It is listening with your whole heart and savoring the moment without rushing to the next.

When we live in the past, we carry regret. When we live in the future, we carry anxiety. Presence is the bridge between both, a sacred space where peace resides. It is not about doing more; it is about being more.

Life is not lived in yesterday or tomorrow; it is lived in this breath, this heartbeat, this moment. When you are present, you experience life in its fullness: the laughter of a loved one, the warmth of sunlight on your skin, the quiet miracle of simply being alive.

Presence deepens relationships. It turns conversations into connections, meals into rituals, and ordinary moments into sacred ones. It is the difference between hearing and truly listening, between looking and truly seeing.

Without presence, we skim the surface of life, missing the depth that gives it meaning. When you choose presence, you choose peace. You choose to anchor yourself in what is real instead of drifting in the currents of regret or anxiety.

Presence is not passive; it is active engagement with the now. It is the power to say, "This moment matters, and I am here for it."

The Cost of Distraction

Distraction steals more than time; it steals meaning. When we scroll instead of savor, when we rush instead of rest, we trade depth for speed. We become spectators of our own lives, watching instead of living.

The cost of distraction is disconnection: from ourselves, from others, from the divine. It fragments our attention and scatters our souls. We lose the ability to notice the small joys: the way a child laughs, the way the wind feels on our face, the way silence can soothe.

Distraction is seductive because it feels productive, but it leaves us empty. We check our phones while eating, think about work during family time, and plan tomorrow while missing today. In all that busyness, we miss the beauty of being alive.

The modern world is designed to keep us distracted. Notifications demand attention. Advertisements create urgency. Social media feeds endless comparison. Yet beneath the noise, your soul is whispering, "Come back. Be here now."

Every moment spent distracted is a moment you cannot reclaim. Every conversation half listened to is a connection half lived. Every sunset missed while staring at a screen is beauty unseen.

Presence is the antidote. It gathers the scattered pieces of your attention and brings you home to yourself. It reminds you that life is not found in the next notification; it is found in the now.

The Gift of Stillness

Stillness is not empty; it is full of wisdom. When you pause, you hear the whispers of your soul. You notice the beauty in the ordinary: the way sunlight dances on the floor, the rhythm of your breath, the sound of laughter.

Stillness is where clarity blooms. It is where creativity awakens, and peace takes root. In stillness, you discover that you are not your thoughts or your worries; you are the awareness beneath them.

To be still is not to do nothing. It is to be fully alive in the quiet. It is to allow space for insight, for healing, for grace. In a culture of constant motion, stillness is a radical act of self-care.

When you practice stillness, you learn to distinguish between the urgent and the important. You realize that not every email requires an immediate response, not every thought deserves your attention, and not every opportunity is yours to take.

Stillness teaches you that you are enough without doing. Your worth is not measured by productivity. Your value is inherent, not earned. In the quiet, you remember this truth.

Presence transforms chaos into calm and turns fleeting moments into timeless memories. It is not about stopping your life; it is about experiencing it fully. And that experience begins with the courage to be still.

Reflection: A Moment of Truth

I used to live in fast-forward, always planning, always chasing the next goal. My days were a blur of deadlines and notifications. I was so busy making a living that I forgot to make a life.

One evening, I stepped outside just as the sun was setting. For the first time in years, I left my phone inside and simply watched. The sky shifted from gold to crimson to deep purple. I felt my breath slow, my shoulders drop, my mind quiet.

In that stillness, I realized something profound: life was not waiting for me at the finish line; it was here, in the quiet glow of a sunset I almost missed. All my rushing had not brought me closer to happiness. It had only taken me further from presence.

That evening changed me. I began practicing small moments of stillness, morning coffee without scrolling, walks without earbuds, and conversations without checking the time. And slowly, I came back to life. Not a different life, but the one I had been living too fast to notice.

Wisdom to Carry Forward

"The present moment is filled with joy and happiness. If you are attentive, you will see it. "Thich Nhat Hanh"
"Realize deeply that the present moment is all you ever have." (*Eckhart Tolle}*

"Wherever you are, be all there." (*Jim Elliot*)

Affirmation

I choose to be fully here. I honor this moment. Presence is my power.

Journal Prompts

- What moments did I rush through today without noticing?
- How does it feel in my body when I am fully present?
- What practices help me return to the now?
- Where in my life do I need more stillness?
- What am I afraid of experiencing if I slow down?

Soul Practice: The Five Senses Ritual

1. Pause wherever you are. Set aside five minutes with no distractions.
2. Engage each sense mindfully:

   - **Sight:** Notice five things you can see—colors, textures, shapes.
   - **Sound:** Listen for four things you can hear, the softest sounds, the furthest sounds.
   - **Touch:** Feel three things: the texture of your clothes, the ground beneath your feet, the air on your skin.

- **Smell:** Identify two scents, even subtle ones, your own skin, the air, a lingering fragrance.
- **Taste:** Notice one taste in your mouth, or mindfully taste something: water, a piece of fruit.

2. Return to this practice whenever you feel scattered or anxious. It brings you home to the present moment.

Guided Meditation

Close your eyes. Take a deep breath. Let your body settle into this moment.

Imagine roots growing from your feet deep into the earth, anchoring you here, now. Feel them spreading, strong and steady.

Feel the air on your skin, the temperature, the subtle movement.

Notice the rhythm of your breath. Not controlling it, just observing. In. Out. In. Out.

Whisper softly to yourself: "I am here. I am whole. I am enough."

If your mind wanders to the past or future, gently guide it back. No judgment. Just return.

Stay in this stillness. Let it fill you. Let it heal you.

There is nowhere else you need to be. Nothing else you need to do. You are exactly where you need to be.

When ready, open your eyes. Carry this presence with you.

Insight to Carry Forward

Presence is not something you find; it is something you choose. Each time you pause, breathe, and notice, you reclaim your life. The power of presence is the power to live truly. The next chapter opens your heart to gratitude, the practice that transforms how you see everything.

CHAPTER 9
The Art of Gratitude Why Gratitude Matters

Gratitude is more than saying "thank you"; it is a way of seeing the world. It shifts your focus from what is missing to what is present, from scarcity to abundance. Gratitude is the lens that reveals beauty in the ordinary and hope in the hard places.

When life feels heavy, gratitude is the anchor that steadies your soul. It does not erase pain, but it reminds you that even in the storm, there is light. Gratitude is not a reaction; it is a practice, a daily choice to notice, to honor, to celebrate.

Gratitude matters because it changes everything: your mood, your mindset, your relationships, even your health. When you practice gratitude, you train your mind to look for blessings instead of burdens. This shift is powerful because what you focus on expands.

Science confirms this truth: gratitude activates the brain's reward system, reduces stress hormones, and boosts resilience. People who practice gratitude regularly report higher levels of happiness and lower levels of anxiety and depression.

But beyond science, gratitude is spiritual medicine. It softens the heart, strengthens relationships, and opens the door to peace. Gratitude moves you from "I need more" to "I have enough." It stops the endless chase for happiness and roots you in the joy of what already is.

Gratitude turns ordinary moments into sacred experiences: a smile, a sunrise, a shared meal. It is not just an emotion; it is a way of living that transforms how you see the world.

The Weight of Ingratitude

When gratitude is absent, life feels like a race we can never win. We measure worth by what we lack, and joy becomes conditional, always waiting for the next achievement, the next possession, the next validation. Ingratitude breeds comparison, and comparison steals contentment.

Without gratitude, we overlook the sacred in the simple, the laughter of a child, the warmth of a meal, the gift of breath. We become blind to the blessings that surround us every day. Ingratitude creates a mindset of scarcity, whispering: "It is not enough. You are not enough."

The weight of ingratitude is heavy because it keeps us focused on what is missing instead of what is present. It robs us of peace and blinds us to beauty. We scroll past moments that could fill us, searching for something better, something more.

Ingratitude also distances us from others. When we cannot appreciate what we have, we cannot truly appreciate who we have. Relationships suffer when we focus on what someone is not giving us rather than celebrating what they are.

This is not about toxic positivity or pretending everything is perfect. It is about recognizing that even in imperfection, there is something to honor. Even in difficulty, there is something to learn. Even in darkness, there is a flicker of light.

Gratitude is the antidote; it lifts the weight and opens our eyes to the abundance that was there all along.

The Transformative Power of Gratitude

Gratitude transforms because it changes the story you tell yourself. Instead of "I am behind," you say, "I am blessed."

Instead of "I have nothing," you whisper, "I have enough." Gratitude does not change circumstances; it changes perspective.

When you live with gratitude, you live with grace. You see abundance where others see lack. You find joy in the smallest details: a smile, a sunrise, a quiet moment of peace. Gratitude turns obstacles into opportunities and pain into purpose.

It is the art of turning ordinary days into sacred celebrations. A meal becomes communion. A conversation becomes a connection. A breath becomes a gift. Gratitude does not require perfect circumstances; it creates beauty within any circumstance.

Gratitude is not passive; it is active. It requires intention, awareness, and practice. But the reward is profound: a life anchored in appreciation, a heart that sees beauty everywhere, and a soul that feels full even when life feels uncertain.

When you practice gratitude, you become a magnet for more goodness, not because the universe is rewarding you, but because you have trained your eyes to see what was always there. Joy begets joy. Appreciation begets appreciation.

This is the alchemy of gratitude: it takes the lead of your life and transforms it into gold.

Reflection: A Moment of Truth

There was a season when I felt stuck; nothing seemed to move forward. My career felt stagnant, relationships felt strained, and each day felt like pushing a boulder uphill.

A wise friend suggested I begin a gratitude practice. I resisted at first. How could I be grateful when so much felt wrong? Yet, I was desperate enough to try.

One morning, I wrote down three things: a warm cup of tea, the sound of birds outside my window, and the kindness of a stranger who held the door. At first, it felt small, almost silly.

Over time, those daily lists became lifelines. They reminded me that even while waiting, life was still beautiful. Gratitude did not change my circumstances overnight, but it changed me.

I noticed more. I complained less. I smiled more easily. Slowly, imperceptibly, my life began to shift, not because everything suddenly went right, but because I learned to see the rightness that was already there.

Wisdom to Carry Forward

"Gratitude turns what we have into enough." "(*Anonymous*)

"Acknowledging the good that you already have in your life is the foundation for all abundance." (*Eckhart Tolle*)

"Gratitude is not only the greatest of virtues, but the parent of all others." (*Cicero)*

Affirmation

I choose gratitude. I see blessings everywhere. My heart is full of thanks.

Journal Prompts

Reflect deeply on these questions:

- What three things am I grateful for today?
- How has gratitude shifted my perspective in the past?
- Who in my life deserves a word of thanks right now?
- How can I make gratitude a daily ritual?
- What blessings have I been taking for granted?

Soul Practice

The Gratitude Jar

This practice creates a tangible collection of blessings.

1. Find a jar or container, something beautiful, if possible.
2. Each day, write one thing you are grateful for on a slip of paper. Be specific: not just "my family," but "the way my daughter laughed at dinner tonight."

3. Place the slip in the jar.

4. At the end of the month (or whenever you need encouragement), empty the jar and read all the gratitude.

5. Notice how abundance has grown in your awareness and how many moments of beauty you almost missed.

6. Keep this practice going. On hard days, add a gratitude; on good days, add several. Let the jar remind you that even in difficulty, there is always something to honor.

Guided Meditation

Close your eyes. Take a deep breath and let your body relax.

Picture your heart as a glowing light, warm, golden, radiant.

With each inhale, imagine this light expanding, growing brighter, filling your chest.

As it expands, let gratitude flow through you for your breath, this moment, and your beating heart.

Whisper softly: "Thank you for this breath. Thank you for this moment. Thank you for this life."

Allow the feeling of appreciation to fill your entire being and overflow.

Think of one person you are grateful for. See their face. Feel your love for them.

Send them this light, this gratitude, this blessing.

Stay here as long as you wish, breathing gratitude in and out.

When ready, open your eyes and carry this warmth with you.

Insight to Carry Forward

Gratitude is not a destination; it is a way of traveling. Each time you pause to give thanks, you plant seeds of joy. Those seeds will bloom into a life of abundance and peace. The next chapter invites you to embrace change with courage and step into transformation rather than resist it.

CHAPTER 10
Courage to Change Why Change Matters

Change is the heartbeat of growth. It is the bridge between who you were and who you are becoming. Yet, change often feels uncomfortable because it asks us to leave the familiar and step into the unknown. It requires courage, the kind that whispers: "I trust what is ahead, even if I cannot see it clearly."

Life is a series of seasons, and each season invites transformation. When we resist change, we cling to what is safe but stagnant. When we embrace it, we open the door to possibility.

Change matters because it is the catalyst for growth. Without change, we remain stuck in patterns that no longer serve us. We cling to comfort zones that feel safe but suffocate our potential. Change is the soil where dreams take root and the wind that carries us toward purpose.

Every breakthrough begins with a shift, a decision to release what was and welcome what can be. Change matters because it keeps life dynamic, teaching us resilience, adaptability, and trust. It reminds us that endings are not failures; they are beginnings in disguise.

When you choose change, you choose life. You choose evolution over stagnation, courage over fear. Change matters because it is the only way to become the fullest version of yourself.

The question is not whether change will come; it always does. The question is: Will you resist it, or will you dance with it?

The Fear of Letting Go

We fear change because we fear loss. Letting go feels like surrendering control, like stepping off solid ground into uncertainty. Our minds cling to the familiar, even when it hurts, because it feels predictable.

Fear whispers: "What if you fail?" Courage answers: "What if you fly?" The truth is, holding on to what no longer fits is a heavier burden than the risk of change.

Staying in spaces that shrink you is more dangerous than stepping into the unknown.

We fear letting go of relationships that have run their course, jobs that no longer fulfill us, and versions of ourselves we have outgrown. We fear the empty space that comes after release, not yet trusting that something new can grow there.

But here is what we often forget: nature teaches us that letting go is essential for renewal. Trees release their leaves to survive winter. Snakes shed their skin to grow. The caterpillar dissolves completely before becoming a butterfly.

Letting go is not about abandoning yourself; it is about honoring your growth. It is trusting that what awaits is greater than what you leave behind. It is saying: "I deserve more than comfort; I deserve freedom."

The fear of letting go is really the fear of discovering who you might become. And that discovery is worth the risk.

The Power of Transformation

Transformation is not instant; it is a process. It begins with awareness, moves through discomfort, and blossoms into freedom. Change stretches us, challenges us, and ultimately strengthens us.

When you embrace change, you step into alignment with your highest self. You discover new strengths, perspectives, and possibilities. Transformation is the art of becoming, not perfect, but authentic. It is the courage to say: "I am ready for more."

True transformation is not about erasing who you were; it is about evolving into who you were always meant to be. It is the unfolding of your potential, the awakening of your purpose, and the deep knowing that growth is worth the risk.

Change is uncomfortable because it requires us to live in the in-between, not yet who we are becoming, no longer who we were. This liminal space feels vulnerable. But it is also sacred; it is where transformation happens.

Every time you choose change, you teach yourself that you are capable of more than you imagined. You prove to yourself that fear does not have the final word. You discover that courage is not the absence of fear, but action in its presence.

Transformation is your birthright. You were designed to evolve, to expand, to become. And every ending is actually an invitation to begin again.

Reflection: A Moment of Truth

There was a time when I stayed in a job that drained me because it felt safe. I told myself, "At least I know what to expect." But deep down, I longed for more. My soul was withering in the familiar.

One day, I realized that fear was writing my story. So, I took a leap, I resigned without a clear plan, trusting that something better would come. It was not easy. There were sleepless nights and moments of doubt.

But that decision opened doors I never imagined. Opportunities I never would have pursued appeared. Skills I did not know I had emerged. Most importantly, I rediscovered myself, the part of me that had been dormant for years.

Change did not just alter my career; it transformed my life. I learned that staying in what no longer serves you is far riskier than stepping into the unknown. Because the unknown holds possibilities. The familiar, when outgrown, holds only stagnation.

That leap taught me: I am braver than I believed. And so are you.

Wisdom to Carry Forward

"Be willing to be a beginner every single morning." (*Meister Eckhart*)

"Your life does not get better by chance; it gets better by change." (*Jim Rohn*)

"Courage is not the absence of fear, but the triumph over it." (*Nelson Mandela*)

Affirmation

I welcome change with courage. I trust the process. I am becoming who I am meant to be.

Journal Prompts

Take time to reflect deeply on these questions:

- What changes am I resisting right now, and why?
- What would my life look like if I embraced this change?
- What fears arise when I think about letting go?
- What small step can I take today toward transformation?
- What old version of myself am I ready to release?

Soul Practice

The Release and Renew Ritual

This practice helps you consciously release the old and invite the new.

1. Write down what you need to release on a piece of paper. Be specific: "I release my fear of failure," "I release this toxic relationship," "I release my need for external validation."
2. Speak aloud: "I let go of what no longer serves me. I release this with love and gratitude for what it taught me."
3. Tear the paper into small pieces (or burn it safely) as a symbolic act of letting go.

4. On a new piece of paper, write your intention for your new beginning: "I welcome courage," "I embrace growth," "I trust my path."
5. Place this intention somewhere visible: your mirror, your workspace, your journal.
6. Each time you see it, remember: you have already taken the first step. You have chosen change over stagnation. You have chosen yourself.

Guided Meditation

Close your eyes. Take three deep breaths. Feel your body grounding.

Imagine yourself standing at the edge of a forest path. Behind you is the familiar, all you have known. Ahead is the unknown, where your growth awaits.

Feel the earth beneath your feet, steady and strong. You are supported. You are safe.

Take a deep breath and step forward onto the path. Notice how it feels, perhaps uncertain, perhaps exciting. Whisper softly: "I trust the journey. I trust myself."

See light ahead; golden, warm, inviting. It represents your potential, your purpose, your transformation.

Walk toward it, one step at a time. You do not need to see the entire path. You just need to take the next step.

Let this image fill you with courage. You are capable of this change. When ready, open your eyes. The path is waiting.

Insight to Carry Forward

Change is not something to fear; it is something to embrace. Each step forward is a declaration of courage, a commitment to growth. Trust the process. You are becoming. And with this chapter, you complete the journey of releasing what no longer serves. The next part invites you into cultivation, nurturing the seeds of your authentic life.

PART THREE
Cultivating Your Soul

CHAPTER 11
Living with Intention Why Intention Matters

Living with intention is about more than setting goals; it is about aligning your actions with your deepest values. It is choosing what matters over what distracts, creating a life that feels authentic rather than reactive.

When we live without intention, we drift, pulled by obligations, expectations, and noise. But when we live with intention, we steer our own ship. We move with clarity, purpose, and peace. Intention is the compass that guides us toward meaning.

Intention matters because it is the foundation of a meaningful life. Every action you take, whether conscious or unconscious, shapes the story you are living. Without intention, life becomes reactive. We move through days responding to demands, distractions, and expectations without asking, "Does this align with who I want to be?"

When you live with intention, you reclaim your power. You stop drifting and start directing. Intention acts as a compass, guiding you toward choices that reflect your values and honor your truth. It transforms ordinary routines into sacred rituals by making every decision purposeful.

Intention matters because it creates clarity. It helps you prioritize what matters most and let go of what does not. It turns "I have to" into "I choose to." It reminds you that your time, energy, and attention are precious resources, and you have the right to invest them wisely.

Living with intention is not about perfection; it is about alignment. It is about asking, "Does this serve my growth? Does this reflect my heart?" When you live with intention, you live with meaning, and meaning is what makes life beautiful.

The Cost of Living on Autopilot

Living on autopilot feels deceptively safe. It gives us the illusion of control because routines are predictable. But beneath that comfort lies a hidden cost: a life half-lived. When we stop choosing consciously, we stop truly living.

Autopilot robs us of presence. We wake, work, scroll, sleep, without asking if these rhythms serve us. Days blur into weeks, and weeks into years, leaving us wondering where time went. We become spectators of our own lives, watching instead of participating.

The cost is not just time; it is meaning. Autopilot keeps us chasing what looks good instead of what feels right. It leads to burnout because we say "yes" to everything without asking if it aligns with our values. It breeds emptiness because we confuse activity with purpose.

When we live on autopilot, we miss the sacred in the simple, the laughter of a loved one, the warmth of a meal, the beauty of a sunrise. We trade depth for speed, connection for convenience, and joy for productivity.

The truth is, every moment offers an opportunity to choose. But without intention, we stop choosing and start drifting. And drifting always leads us away from the life we truly want. Waking up from autopilot requires courage. It means pausing to ask, "Is this what I want? Is this who I want to be?" Those questions can feel uncomfortable, but they are also liberating.

The Freedom of Intentional Living

Intentional living is liberating because it frees you from the weight of "should." It releases you from the pressure to meet everyone else's expectations and invites you to honor your own. When you live with intention, you stop chasing approval and start creating authenticity.

Freedom comes from choice, the conscious choice to design your life instead of drifting through it. Intentional living allows you to say "yes" to what nourishes your soul and "no" to what drains it. It permits you to slow down, savor and simplify.

When you live with intention, you experience peace because your actions align with your values. You feel empowered because you are no longer reacting; you are creating. You discover that freedom is not found in doing everything; it is found in doing what matters most.

Intentional living is not rigid; it is fluid. It adapts as you grow, as your priorities shift, as your dreams evolve. It is a lifelong practice of choosing with awareness, loving with purpose, and living with clarity.

Each morning becomes an opportunity to set your compass. Each decision becomes a vote for the life you want to create. Each "no" to what does not serve you is a "yes" to what does.

In that practice, you find the deepest kind of freedom, the freedom to be fully, authentically you.

Reflection: A Moment of Truth

There was a time when my days felt like a blur, meetings, errands, and endless scrolling. I was busy but not fulfilled. Every morning, I woke up and went through my routines without asking whether they mattered. Life felt like a checklist, and I was ticking boxes without joy.

One morning, I sat at my kitchen table, coffee in hand, and asked myself a simple question: "What do I truly want today to feel like?"

That question changed everything. I wrote down three intentions: to speak kindly, to move my body with gratitude, and to savor my meals without distraction.

That day felt different, lighter, richer, and more alive. I noticed the warmth of my coffee instead of gulping it down. I paused before responding to a colleague and chose words that carried grace. I walked outside and felt the sun on my skin.

These were not grand gestures; they were small, conscious choices. But over time, those choices became habits. And those habits became a life that felt aligned.

Living with intention taught me that meaning is not found in doing more; it is found in doing what matters most.

Wisdom to Carry Forward

"When you live with intention, every moment becomes meaningful." (*Unknown*)

"The future depends on what you do today." (*Mahatma Gandhi*).

"Live less out of habit and more out of intent." (*Amy Rubin Flett*).

Affirmation

I choose to live with purpose. My actions reflect my values. My life is intentional and meaningful.

Journal Prompts

Take time to reflect deeply on these questions:

What does living with intention mean to me?

- Which areas of my life feel aligned, and which feel out of sync?
- What three intentions can guide my day tomorrow?
- How can I create space for what matters most?
- What am I doing out of habit that no longer serves me?

Soul Practice

The Daily Intention Ritual

This practice helps you start each day with clarity and purpose.

1. Each morning, before checking your phone or diving into tasks, take five minutes for yourself.
2. Write down one intention for the day. Not a to-do list item, but a way of being. Examples:
3. "Today, I choose presence over productivity."
4. "Today, I speak with kindness to myself and others."
5. "Today, I honor my boundaries."
6. Speak it aloud: "Today, I choose…"
7. Carry it with you, write it on a note, set it as a phone reminder, or simply hold it in your awareness.
8. At the end of the day, reflect: Did my actions align with my intention? What did I learn?

9. Release judgment. Some days you will embody your intention fully. Other days you will forget and remember. Both are part of the practice.

Guided Meditation

Close your eyes. Take three deep breaths. Feel your body settling.

Imagine a clear path stretching before you. This path represents your life, your journey, your days ahead.

Each step you take is guided by light, the light of your values, your dreams, your deepest truth.

See yourself walking this path with intention. Not rushing. Not forcing. Simply moving forward with clarity and purpose.

Whisper softly: "I walk with intention. Each step matters. Each choice creates my life."

Feel the peace of moving with purpose. Feel the power of conscious choice. Stay with this image. Let it fill you with clarity. When ready, open your eyes. Remember: you are the one who chooses the path.

Insight to Carry Forward

Intention is the art of living on purpose. Each choice is a brushstroke on the canvas of your life. Paint with care. Paint with love. Paint with meaning. The next chapter invites you to turn that intentional awareness inward, to practice the revolutionary act of self-compassion.

CHAPTER 12
The Gift of Self-Compassion Why Self-Compassion Matters

Self-compassion is the quiet revolution that changes everything. It is the practice of treating yourself with the same kindness you offer others. In a world that glorifies perfection and productivity, self-compassion feels radical. It whispers: "You are worthy, not because you are flawless, but because you are human."

When we neglect self-compassion, we become our harshest critics. We punish ourselves for mistakes, compare ourselves to others, and measure our worth by impossible standards. But when we embrace it, we create space for healing, growth, and peace.

Self-compassion matters because it is the foundation of emotional, mental, and spiritual well-being. Without it, we live in a constant state of self-judgment, measuring our worth against impossible standards. Life will always bring challenges, mistakes, failures, and disappointments, but how we respond to those moments determines whether we grow or break.

When we meet ourselves with kindness instead of criticism, we create space for healing. Self-compassion is not weakness; it is strength in its purest form. It allows us to acknowledge our humanity, the truth that imperfection is not a flaw but a shared experience.

Research confirms what the heart already knows: people who practice self-compassion experience lower levels of anxiety and depression, greater resilience, and stronger motivation. Why? Because kindness fuels courage. When you know you will not punish yourself for failing, you feel safe to try, to dream, to risk.

Self-compassion matters because it shifts the inner dialogue from "I am not enough" to "I am learning, and that is okay." It transforms shame into growth and fear into freedom. It is the soil where confidence blooms and the light that guides us back to peace.

The Weight of Self-Criticism

Self-criticism is heavy and dangerous. It does not just hurt your feelings; it rewires your brain to expect failure and fear judgment. Every harsh word you speak to yourself becomes a brick in the wall that separates you from joy.

The weight of self-criticism shows up in subtle ways. Emotionally, you feel anxious, ashamed, and never enough. Mentally, you replay mistakes like broken records, magnifying flaws until they define you. Physically, chronic stress from self-criticism raises cortisol levels, weakens the immune system, and drains energy.

Over time, self-criticism erodes confidence and creativity. It silences your voice, shrinks your dreams, and convinces you that failure is fatal. It becomes a cycle: the harsher you are on yourself, the more you fear mistakes, and the more mistakes feel catastrophic.

The inner critic often sounds like voices from your past, a parent, a teacher, a bully, but now you have internalized it. You have become your own oppressor, repeating judgments that were never yours to carry.

The truth is, self-criticism does not make you stronger; it makes you smaller. It does not motivate, it paralyzes. And the longer you carry it, the heavier it becomes, crushing the joy and vitality your soul was meant to hold.

But here is what you need to know: that voice is not your truth. It is an old recording. And you have the power to turn it off.

The Freedom of Self-Compassion

Self-compassion is liberating because it breaks the cycle of shame and perfectionism. It permits you to be human, to rest, to make mistakes, and to grow at your own pace. It turns harsh inner dialogue into gentle truth: "I am learning. I am growing. I am enough."

When you practice self-compassion, you create space for joy. You stop chasing perfection and start embracing progress. You discover that freedom is not found in doing everything right; it is found in loving yourself even when you do not.

Self-compassion does not mean avoiding responsibility; it means approaching responsibility with kindness. It means saying: "I made a mistake, but I am not a mistake." This shift changes everything.

It transforms failure into feedback, shame into strength, and fear into courage. It allows you to show up fully, not because you are flawless, but because you are free.

When you speak to yourself with compassion, you heal old wounds. You rewrite the stories you have been told about your worth. You discover that you have always been deserving of love, not because of what you do, but because of who you are.

Self-compassion is not indulgent; it is essential. It is not soft, it is strong. It is the practice that transforms your relationship with yourself and, in doing so, your entire life.

Reflection: A Moment of Truth

I remember a client named Sarah, a brilliant and hardworking woman who carried the weight of perfection on her shoulders. Sarah believed that being hard on herself was the key to success. Every mistake was magnified in her mind, every flaw became a reason to push harder.

One day, after missing a deadline, she stayed up all night rewriting reports, berating herself for being "lazy" and "careless." Over time, that inner harshness began to show. Her smile faded, her energy drained, and her confidence crumbled.

After a particularly difficult week, Sarah broke down and admitted, "I do not know how to be kind to myself."

That moment was a turning point. With support, she began practicing small acts of self-compassion, speaking gently to herself, taking breaks without guilt, and celebrating progress instead of perfection.

Months later, Sarah was different. She still worked hard, but her energy was lighter, her laughter returned, and her confidence grew, not because she became flawless, but because she learned to love herself through her flaws.

Self-compassion did not make her weaker; it made her unstoppable.

Wisdom to Carry Forward

"Talk to yourself like you would to someone you love." (*Brené Brown*)

"You have been criticizing yourself for years, and it has not worked. Try approving of yourself and see what happens." (*Louise Hay*)

"Self-compassion is simply giving the same kindness to ourselves that we would give to others." (*Christopher Germer*)

Affirmation

I choose kindness toward myself. I release judgment. I am worthy of love and grace.

Journal Prompts

Take time to reflect deeply on these questions:

- What harsh words do I often say to myself?
- How can I reframe those words with compassion?
- What would I say to a friend in my situation, and can I say that to myself?
- What does loving myself look like today?
- When did I first learn to criticize myself? Who taught me this?

Soul Practice

The Self-Compassion Letter

This practice helps you speak to yourself with the kindness you deserve.

1. Think of a mistake you made or a struggle you are facing. Notice how you feel about it.
2. Now, imagine a dear friend came to you with the same struggle. What would you say to them?
3. Write a letter to yourself as if you were writing to that friend. Begin with: "Dear [Your Name], I see that you are struggling with…"
4. Offer yourself encouragement, forgiveness, understanding, and love. Be as kind as you would be to someone you care about deeply.
5. Read the letter aloud to yourself. Let the words sink in. Notice how your body feels.
6. Keep this letter. Return to it on difficult days. You deserve these words, always.

Guided Meditation

Close your eyes. Place your hand over your heart. Feel it beating beneath your palm.

Take a deep breath. Let your body soften.

Whisper softly to yourself: "I am enough. I am loved. I am learning."

Feel warmth spreading through your chest, melting tension, and filling you with peace.

Imagine someone you love standing before you. See the compassion in their eyes. Now, turn that compassion toward yourself.

Repeat: "I forgive myself. I accept myself. I am worthy of my own kindness."

Stay with this feeling. Let it grow. Let it heal.

When ready, open your eyes. Carry this compassion with you.

Insight to Carry Forward

Self-compassion is not indulgent; it is essential. It is the foundation of healing, growth, and joy. Each time you choose kindness over judgment, you choose freedom. The next chapter invites you to release the need for control and discover the beauty of surrender.

CHAPTER 13
The Beauty of Surrender Why Surrender Matters

Surrender is not giving up; it is letting go of the illusion that we can control everything. It is the quiet courage to release what we cannot change and trust what we cannot see. In a world that glorifies control, surrender feels counterintuitive. Yet, it is the doorway to peace.

When we cling tightly, we exhaust ourselves trying to force outcomes. But when we surrender, we create space for grace. We allow life to unfold in ways we could never orchestrate. Surrender is not weakness; it is wisdom. It whispers, "I trust the timing. I trust the process. I trust that what is meant for me will find me."

Surrender matters because it is the ultimate act of empowerment. It is choosing trust over fear, peace over panic, and faith over control. Control is an illusion; no matter how hard we try, we cannot dictate every outcome. The more we cling, the more we suffer.

When you surrender, you are not abandoning your dreams; you are releasing the anxiety that comes from trying to force them. You are saying: "I have done my part, and now I allow life to do its part." This is not passive; it is active trust. It is courage in its purest form.

Surrender matters because it frees you from the exhausting cycle of "what if." It allows you to live in the present rather than obsess over the future. It teaches you that peace is not found in certainty; it is found in trust.

When you surrender, you open the door to possibilities you could never imagine. You create space for grace, unexpected blessings and divine timing. Surrender is not weakness; it is strength. It is the strength to release what was never yours to carry and embrace what is meant for you.

The Weight of Control

Control feels safe, but it is heavy, like carrying a backpack filled with stones you never needed to pick up. We cling to control because it gives us the illusion of certainty. We believe that if we plan enough, predict enough, and prepare enough, we can avoid pain and guarantee success. But the truth is, control is exhausting.

The weight of control shows up in sleepless nights spent replaying conversations, in the tension that knots your shoulders as you try to manage every detail, and in the anxiety that whispers: "What if something goes wrong?" It robs us of presence because we are always living in the "what if" instead of the "what is."

Control convinces us that perfection is possible if we just try harder. But perfection is a mirage, and chasing it only leads to burnout. The harder we grip, the more life resists. And in that resistance, we lose peace, joy, and clarity.

We try to control outcomes in relationships, how people respond, how they feel, whether they stay or leave. We try to control our careers, every step, every timeline, every possibility. We try to control our healing, how fast, how perfect, how pain-free.

But control is an illusion. Life is fluid. People are complex. Timing is mysterious. And the more we try to force things to bend to our will, the more we break ourselves in the process.

The weight of control keeps us from experiencing life as it unfolds. We miss the beauty of spontaneity, the gifts in detours, and the wisdom in waiting. We become so focused on what we think should happen that we cannot see what is happening.

And beneath all that control? Fear. Fear of the unknown. Fear of failure. Fear of not being enough. Control is not strength; it is fear dressed up in urgency.

The Freedom of Letting Go

Letting go is liberating because it releases the burden of trying to manage what is beyond our reach. It is the moment you exhale after holding your breath for too long. It is the quiet courage to say: "I have done my part. Now I release the rest."

Letting go does not mean giving up; it means permitting yourself to trust. It means choosing faith over fear and peace over panic. When you let go, you create space for grace, unexpected blessings, divine timing and possibilities you could never imagine.

Freedom comes when you stop fighting life and start flowing with it. It is not passive; it is active trust. It is the strength to loosen your grip and believe that what is meant for you will find you. In letting go, you discover that life often works out better than you could ever plan.

Surrender teaches you that you are not in control, and that is okay. You are held. You are guided. You are supported by something greater than your own effort. When you release your grip, you allow that support to carry you.

Letting go looks different for everyone. For some, it is releasing a relationship that has run its course. For others, it is releasing the need to know how everything will unfold. For still others, it is releasing the story of who they thought they should be and embracing who they actually are.

But in every case, letting go brings relief. The tight knot in your chest loosens. The constant mental chatter quiets. The exhaustion lifts. You realize that you were carrying a burden you were never meant to carry.

And in that space, the space created by letting go, new life grows. New dreams emerge. New paths reveal themselves. Because surrender is not an ending, it is a beginning.

Reflection: A Moment of Truth

I once knew someone who spent years trying to control every detail of life, career, relationships, and even timing. Every plan was mapped out, every risk calculated. They believed that control was the key to security. But life had other plans.

A sudden job loss shattered the illusion of control. At first, there was panic, endless nights of worry, frantic attempts to fix everything, and desperate efforts to force things back into place.

Then, slowly, something shifted. Instead of forcing the next step, they paused. They breathed. They trusted. It was not easy letting go, never is, but in that space of surrender, something miraculous happened.

Opportunities appeared that they had never considered. A new career path opened, one that aligned more deeply with their passions than anything they had planned. Relationships deepened because they stopped trying to script every outcome and started showing up authentically.

Months later, they said to me, "Losing control was the best thing that ever happened to me. It taught me that life works out, not because I control it, but because I trust it."

Surrender did not mean giving up; it meant gaining freedom. It meant discovering that peace is found not in holding on, but in letting go.

Wisdom to Carry Forward

- "Sometimes letting things go is an act of far greater power than defending or hanging on." (*Eckhart Tolle*)
- "Surrender is the simple but profound wisdom of yielding to rather than opposing the flow of life." (*Eckhart Tolle*)
- "Let go and let life surprise you." (*Unknown*)

Affirmation

I release what I cannot control. I trust the process. Peace flows through me.

Journal Prompts

Take time to reflect deeply on these questions:

- What am I holding onto that feels heavy?
- What would it feel like to let this go?
- Where in my life do I need more trust?

- How can surrender bring me peace today?
- What outcome am I trying to force that needs to be released?

Soul Practice

The River Release Ritual

This practice helps you consciously release control and embrace surrender.

1. Write down what you need to surrender on a piece of paper. Be specific and honest:

   - "I surrender my need to control how others see me."
   - "I surrender the timeline I have created for my healing."
   - "I surrender the outcome of this situation."

2. Hold the paper in your hands. Feel the weight of what you have been carrying.
3. Speak aloud: "I release this with trust. I surrender this with faith. I let go with grace."
4. If possible, place the paper in flowing water (a stream, river, or ocean) and watch it dissolve or drift away. If not near water, tear it into small pieces and release them to the wind, or burn it safely as a symbolic act of letting go.
5. As you release it, visualize the burden lifting from your shoulders. Feel the lightness. Feel the freedom.

6. Place your hand on your heart and whisper: "I trust. I am held. I am free."

Guided Meditation

Close your eyes. Take three deep breaths. Feel your body grounding.

Imagine yourself standing by a river. The water flows gently, steadily, endlessly. This river represents the flow of life; constant, unstoppable, beyond your control.

In your hands, you hold a stone; heavy, solid. This stone represents what you have been trying to control. Feel its weight.

Notice how tiring it is to hold this stone. How long have you been carrying it? How much energy has it taken?

Now, slowly, walk to the edge of the river. Kneel down. Hold the stone over the water.

Whisper: "I release this. I trust the river. I surrender to the flow."

Let the stone drop into the water. Watch it sink. Watch the ripples spread and then disappear. The river continues flowing, unchanged, eternal.

Feel the lightness in your hands. Feel the space where the burden used to be.

Place both hands on your heart and repeat: "I let go. I trust."

Stay by the river as long as you need. When you are ready, open your eyes.

Remember: the river knows where it is going. You do not need to control it. You only need to flow with it.

Insight to Carry Forward

Surrender is not defeat; it is freedom. It is the art of trusting life's timing and releasing what was never yours to carry. Each time you let go, you make room for grace. The next chapter invites you to discover another form of freedom, the power of sacred boundaries that protect your peace and honor your worth.

CHAPTER 14
Nurturing Sacred Boundaries Why Boundaries Matter

Boundaries are not walls; they are bridges to healthier relationships. They are the loving limits you set to protect your energy, honor your needs, and preserve your peace. In a world that often demands more than you can give, boundaries are your lifeline to sustainability and self-respect.

When you honor your boundaries, you teach others how to honor you. When you ignore them, you teach others that your needs do not matter. Boundaries are not selfish; they are sacred. They are the declaration that your well-being matters, your time is valuable, and your peace is worth protecting.

Boundaries matter because they are the foundation of healthy relationships, with others and with yourself. Without boundaries, resentment builds, burnout looms, and authenticity suffers. You find yourself saying yes when you mean no, giving when you have nothing left, and sacrificing your well-being for others' comfort.

Healthy boundaries do not push people away; they invite authentic connection. When you are clear about your limits, people know where they stand with you. There is no guessing, no manipulation, and no silent resentment. Just honest, respectful engagement.

Boundaries teach others how to love you well. They say: "This is what I need to thrive. This is what honors my worth. This is what allows me to show up as my best self." And the people who truly care about you will respect those boundaries, not resent them.

Without boundaries, you become a vessel constantly being poured out, never refilled. With boundaries, you become a well, deep, nourished, able to give from overflow rather than depletion. This is not selfishness. This is sustainability. This is wisdom.

The Cost of Weak Boundaries

Weak boundaries are expensive. They cost you your energy, your peace, your authenticity, and eventually, your health. When you consistently override your own needs to accommodate others, you send your soul the message: "You do not matter."

The cost shows up in subtle ways at first. You feel tired but cannot explain why. You feel resentful but do not know toward whom. You feel suffocated but cannot identify what is taking your breath. These are the whispers of boundaries ignored.

Over time, weak boundaries lead to burnout. You give and give until you have nothing left. You take care of everyone except yourself. You become the last priority on your own list. And when you finally collapse from exhaustion, you wonder how you got here.

Weak boundaries also damage relationships. When you cannot say no, your yes loses meaning. When you hide your true feelings to keep the peace, the connection becomes shallow. When you accommodate everyone else, people never learn who you really are.

Resentment is the toll of weak boundaries. Every time you say yes when you mean no, resentment grows. Every time you sacrifice your needs to avoid conflict, bitterness accumulates. And one day, that resentment erupts, often at someone who had no idea they were crossing a line because you never drew one.

The cost of weak boundaries is also physical. Chronic stress from overextending yourself can affect your immune system, sleep, digestion, and overall health. Your body keeps the score of every boundary violation, including the ones you commit against yourself.

But perhaps the highest cost is this: weak boundaries disconnect you from yourself. You become so focused on what everyone else needs that you forget what you need. You become so skilled at reading others that you lose the ability to read yourself. You become a stranger in your own life.

The Gift of Strong Boundaries

Strong boundaries are liberating. They free you from the exhausting performance of people-pleasing. They create space for authentic relationships where you can show up as yourself, not as who others need you to be.

When you honor your boundaries, you reclaim your energy. You stop giving from depletion and start giving from overflow. You discover that you have more to offer when you are not running on empty. Your presence becomes a gift instead of an obligation.

Strong boundaries also protect your peace. They filter out what does not serve you: toxic relationships, draining commitments, obligations that feel heavy rather than aligned. They create a sanctuary within your life where you can rest, recharge, and reconnect with yourself.

Boundaries are an act of self-love. They say: "I am worthy of respect, starting with my own." They demonstrate that you value yourself enough to protect your well-being. And that self-valuing is magnetic. It attracts people who respect boundaries and repels those who do not.

The gift of boundaries is also clarity. When you know your limits, decision-making becomes easier. You can quickly discern what a yes is and what a no is. You stop agonizing over choices because your boundaries provide a framework for alignment.

Strong boundaries do not make you rigid; they make you resilient. They give you the strength to bend without breaking, to be flexible without losing yourself, to adapt without abandoning your core values.

And here is the beautiful truth: when you honor your boundaries, you permit others to honor theirs. You create a culture of respect, authenticity, and mutual care. You model what healthy relationships look like. You become a safe space for others to be themselves, because you are finally safe to be yourself.

Reflection: A Moment of Truth

I once worked with a client who was the go-to person for everyone. Family, friends, colleagues, they all knew they could count on her. She wore her helpfulness like a badge of honor, never saying no, always available, perpetually giving.

But one day, she came to our session in tears. "I am so tired," she said. "I feel like I am drowning, but I do not know how to stop."

As we explored her life, the pattern became clear: she had no boundaries. Every request was automatically a yes. Every need except her own was immediately met. She had confused love with martyrdom, service with self-sacrifice.

When I asked, "What would happen if you said no?" her eyes widened in fear. "They would be disappointed. They would think I do not care. They might leave."

That fear, of disappointing others, of being seen as selfish, of being abandoned, had kept her imprisoned in a pattern of self-neglect. So, we started small. One at a time. One boundary at a time. One act of self-honoring at a time.

At first, it felt terrifying. But then something remarkable happened. Most people respected her boundaries. And those who did not? They revealed themselves as people who only valued her for what she could give, not for who she was.

Six months later, she was transformed. Not exhausted, but energized. Not resentful, but at peace. Not people-pleasing, but authentically connecting. She had learned that boundaries are not barriers to love; they are the foundation of it.

Wisdom to Carry Forward

"Daring to set boundaries is about having the courage to love ourselves, even when we risk disappointing others." Brené Brown

"No is a complete sentence." (*Anne Lamott*)

"Boundaries are a part of self-care. They are healthy, normal, and necessary." (*Doreen Virtue*)

Affirmation

I honor my boundaries. I protect my energy. I say no with love and yes with clarity.

Journal Prompts

Take time to reflect deeply on these questions:

- Where in my life do I need stronger boundaries?
- What happens when I do not honor my limits?
- What would it feel like to say no without guilt?
- How can I communicate my boundaries with compassion?
- Who in my life respects my boundaries, and who does not?

Soul Practice

Boundary Mapping Exercise

This practice helps you identify where boundaries are needed and how to set them.

1. **Reflect on Different Life Areas:** Draw four circles on a page labeled Relationships, Work, Personal Time and Energy.
2. For Each Area, Ask:

- Where do I feel drained?

- Where do I say yes when I want to say no?
- Where do I feel resentful?
- Where am I overextending?

3. Identify One Boundary You Need in Each Area. Examples:

   - Relationships: "I will not answer phone calls after 9 PM."
   - Work: "I will not check email on weekends."
   - Personal Time: "I will protect one hour each day for myself."
   - Energy: "I will say no to obligations that deplete me."

4. Write a Script for Setting Each Boundary:

   - "I care about you, and I also need to honor my rest. I am not available after 9 PM, but I would love to talk tomorrow."
   - "I value my work, and I also value my personal time. I will respond to your email on Monday."

5. **Practice Saying It:** Stand in front of a mirror and speak your boundary aloud. Notice how it feels. Adjust the words until they feel authentic.

6. **Commit to One Boundary This Week:** Start small. Honor one boundary consistently. Notice what changes.

Guided Meditation

Close your eyes. Take three deep breaths. Feel your body settling.

Imagine yourself surrounded by a gentle, glowing light. This light represents your sacred space, your energy, your peace, your well-being.

Notice how beautiful and calm this space feels. It is yours. It is safe. It is protected.

Now imagine that this light has a boundary, a soft, permeable membrane that lets in love, respect, and authentic connection, but filters out demands, manipulation, and energy drain.

Feel the security of this boundary. It does not isolate you; it protects you. It does not push people away; it invites healthy connections.

Whisper to yourself: "I am worthy of boundaries. My needs matter. My peace is sacred."

See this boundary growing stronger, clearer. You are in control of who and what enters your sacred space.

Place your hand on your heart and repeat: "I honor my boundaries. I protect my energy. I choose me."

Stay here as long as you need. When ready, open your eyes, knowing that your boundaries are yours to set and yours to honor.

Insight to Carry Forward

Boundaries are not walls; they are bridges to healthier relationships. They honor your worth and protect your peace. Every time you uphold a boundary, you choose yourself. You choose sustainability. You choose love, real love, not codependence. The next chapter invites you to deepen your trust in the wisdom that has always lived within you, your inner knowing, your intuition, your self-trust.

CHAPTER 15
The Alchemy of Self-Trust Why Self-Trust Matters

Self-trust is the foundation of everything, every decision, every relationship, every dream. It is the quiet confidence that whispers: "I can trust myself to handle what comes." Without it, we second-guess every choice, seek validation from everyone else, and live paralyzed by fear of making the wrong move.

When you trust yourself, you move through life with clarity and courage. You do not need endless opinions or perfect certainty. You listen to your inner wisdom and trust that you will figure it out. Self-trust is not arrogance; it is humility. It is knowing you are capable while remaining open to growth.

Self-trust matters because it is the key to freedom. When you trust yourself, you stop outsourcing your decisions to others. You stop waiting for permission to live your life. You stop doubting your worthiness and start owning your power.

Without self-trust, you remain stuck, afraid to move forward, afraid to make mistakes, afraid to disappoint. You spend more time questioning yourself than living. You defer to others because you believe they know better. You abandon your intuition because you think it cannot be trusted.

But here is the truth: you have always known. Deep down, beneath the noise, the doubt, and the fear, you have always known what is right for you. Self-trust is simply the practice of listening to that knowing and honoring it.

When you trust yourself, you reclaim your power. You become the author of your story, not a character in someone else's. You make decisions aligned with your values, not dictated by fear. You show up authentically because you trust that who you are is enough.

The Erosion of Self-Trust

Self-trust is not lost overnight; it erodes slowly through years of small betrayals. Every time you ignore your intuition and something goes wrong, trust weakens. Every time you abandon your needs to please others, trust fractures. Every time you silence your voice to keep the peace, trust fades.

Self-trust erodes when others dismiss your feelings: "You are too sensitive." "You are overreacting." "That is not what happened." Over time, you begin to doubt your own perception. You question your reality. You wonder if you can trust your own mind.

It erodes when you make promises to yourself and break them. When you say you will set boundaries but do not. When you commit to self-care but abandon it when things get busy, each broken promise to yourself sends a message: "I cannot count on myself."

Trauma also erodes self-trust. When your body or mind reacts in ways you do not understand, when you feel out of control, when you cannot protect yourself, your trust in your own capacity to handle life diminishes. You begin to see yourself as fragile, incapable, or broken.

The erosion of self-trust creates anxiety. If you cannot trust yourself, who can you trust? You become hyper-vigilant, always scanning for danger, always questioning your choices, always seeking reassurance from others. But no amount of external validation can fill the void of self-trust.

The good news? Self-trust can be rebuilt. Just as it was lost through small betrayals, it can be restored through small acts of honoring yourself. Every time you listen to your intuition, every time you keep a promise to yourself, every time you choose your truth over approval, you rebuild trust, one choice at a time.

Rebuilding Self-Trust

Rebuilding self-trust begins with listening; listening to the whispers of your intuition, the wisdom of your body, the truth of your emotions. Your inner knowing has been there all along, patiently waiting for you to return.

Start small. Make a promise to yourself and keep it: "I will go to bed by 10 PM tonight." "I will take a walk this afternoon." "I will honor my no." Each kept promise is a deposit in the bank of self-trust. Over time, those deposits compound, and you begin to see yourself as someone who follows through.

Rebuilding self-trust also means honoring your feelings. When you feel uneasy about something, do not dismiss it. Investigate it. Your discomfort is information. When you feel drawn to something, explore it. Your desire is a compass. Trust that your feelings are valid, even if others do not understand them.

Self-trust grows through self-reflection. After making a decision, reflect on the outcome without judgment. If it worked out, celebrate. If it did not, ask: "What did I learn?" Every experience, successful or not, is a teacher. When you view mistakes as lessons rather than failures, your trust in your ability to navigate life strengthens.

Practice self-compassion as you rebuild trust. You will stumble. You will doubt yourself. You will make mistakes. That is part of being human. The goal is not perfection, it is progress. Each time you choose to trust yourself, even imperfectly, you strengthen that muscle.

Surround yourself with people who honor your knowing, people who ask, "What do you think?" instead of telling you what to do. People who respect your choices even when they would choose differently. These relationships reinforce the message: "You are capable. You can trust yourself."

Self-trust is alchemy; it transforms fear into courage, doubt into clarity, and hesitation into action. It is the bridge between who you were and who you are becoming. And it begins with one simple choice: to believe in yourself again.

Reflection: A Moment of Truth

There was a time when I could not trust my own judgment. I had made a decision that did not turn out as I hoped, and the fallout was painful. For years afterward, I questioned every choice. I sought advice from everyone around me, paralyzed by fear of making another mistake.

One day, a mentor asked me: "What does your gut tell you?" I stared blankly. I had been ignoring my gut for so long that I could no longer hear it. She smiled gently and said, "It is still there. You just need to get quiet enough to listen."

So, I began practicing small decisions at first. "What do I want for lunch?" "Which route should I take home?" I stopped asking others and started asking myself. At first, it felt uncomfortable, like using a muscle that had atrophied. But slowly, I started to hear the whispers again.

The more I listened, the louder the whispers became. And the more I honored them, the more I trusted myself. I realized that the mistake I had made years ago was not proof that I could not be trusted; it was proof that I was human. And humans grow through mistakes.

Today, I trust myself. Not because I am perfect, but because I know I can handle whatever comes. I know that even if I make a mistake, I will learn from it. I know that my intuition is wise, my feelings are valid, and my choices are mine to make.

Self-trust did not return overnight. But it did return. And it can for you, too.

Wisdom to Carry Forward

"Trust yourself. You know more than you think you do." (*Benjamin Spock*)

"The more you trust yourself, the less you compare yourself to others." (*Roy T. Bennett*)

"Self-trust is the first secret of success." (*Ralph Waldo Emerson*)

Affirmation

I trust myself. I honor my intuition. I am capable of navigating my life with wisdom and grace.

Journal Prompts

- Take time to reflect deeply on these questions:
- When have I ignored my intuition and later regretted it?
- What small promise can I make to myself today and keep?
- Where in my life do I seek external validation instead of trusting myself?
- What would change if I fully trusted my inner knowing?
- How can I practice self-compassion as I rebuild self-trust?

Soul Practice: The Self-Trust Journal

This practice helps you reconnect with and strengthen your inner knowing.

1. Each day, write down one decision you made—big or small. Examples:

    - "I chose to have tea instead of coffee."
    - "I said no to an invitation that did not feel aligned."

- "I spoke up in a meeting when I had an idea."

1. Reflect on the decision:

   - What did my intuition say?
   - Did I honor it or ignore it?
   - How did the outcome feel?

1. Celebrate decisions you trusted yourself on, regardless of the outcome. Write: "I trusted myself today by..."
2. For decisions where you ignored yourself, ask: "What was I afraid of?" and "How can I honor my knowing next time?"
3. At the end of each week, review your entries. Notice patterns. Notice growth. Notice the increasing strength of your self-trust.
4. Add a weekly reflection: "This week, I am proud of myself for trusting..."

Guided Meditation

Close your eyes. Take three deep breaths. Feel your body becoming still.

Place both hands over your heart. Feel it beating; steady, reliable, constant. This is your center. This is your truth.

Imagine a warm, golden light glowing in your chest. This light is your inner knowing, your intuition, your wisdom, your truth.

Feel it pulsing gently, radiating warmth throughout your body. It has always been there, waiting for you to return.

Whisper softly: "I trust you. I hear you. I honor you."

Ask your inner knowing a question: "What do I need to know right now?"

Listen, not with your mind, but with your heart. The answer may come as words, feelings, images, or simply a sense of knowing.

Whatever arises, receive it without judgment. Trust it.

Repeat: "I trust myself. I am wise. I am capable."

Feel the golden light growing brighter and stronger, filling your entire being with confidence and clarity.

When ready, open your eyes. Carry this light with you. It is always there, always guiding you home to yourself.

Insight to Carry Forward

Self-trust is not something you find; it is something you rebuild, one choice at a time. Every time you honor your intuition, keep a promise to yourself, or choose your truth, you strengthen that trust. And with that trust comes freedom, the freedom to live as you are meant to live.

You have completed Part Three: *Cultivating Your Soul.* Now, you are ready for the final journey, Part Four.

Embodying Your Purpose. This is where everything you have learned comes together as you step fully into the life your soul has been calling you toward.

PART FOUR
Embodying Your Purpose

CHAPTER 16
Awakening Your Life Purpose Why Purpose Matters

Purpose is not something you find in a single moment of revelation. It is something you awaken to through living, learning, and listening to your soul. It is the deeper reason you are here, the unique contribution only you can make, and the legacy your life will leave.

When you live with purpose, everything changes. Work becomes meaningful. Relationships deepen. Challenges become pathways for growth. You move through life with direction, clarity, and a sense of belonging to something greater than yourself.

Purpose matters because it answers the soul's most persistent question: "Why am I here?" Without purpose, life can feel like moving through the motions; days that blur together, achievements that feel hollow, success that leaves you empty. With purpose, every moment matters. Every choice carries meaning. Every day contributes to something significant.

Living with purpose does not mean having all the answers. It means being willing to ask the questions. It means paying attention to what lights you up, what breaks your heart, and what you cannot stop thinking about. Purpose emerges when passion meets pain, when your gifts meet the world's needs, and when your joy meets someone else's healing.

Purpose is not always grand or world-changing. Sometimes it is quiet and intimate, raising children with intention, creating beauty through art, serving your community, or listening deeply to those who feel unheard. Purpose is not measured by impact. It is measured by alignment. Are you living in harmony with who you truly are?

When you awaken to your purpose, you stop living by default and start living by design. You stop asking, "What should I do?" and start asking, "What am I called to do?" You stop seeking approval and start seeking authenticity. You stop comparing your path to others and start trusting your own. Purpose becomes the North Star that guides you home to yourself.

The Search for Meaning

The search for meaning is an ancient and universal phenomenon. Every human soul longs to know: "Does my life matter? Am I making a difference? Will I be remembered?" These questions are not signs of insecurity. They are signs of awakening. They are the soul's invitation to step into something deeper.

Many people spend decades chasing external markers of success, money, status, and recognition, hoping these will bring meaning. But external achievements, while valuable, cannot fill the void of purposelessness. You can have everything the world says you should want and still feel empty if you are not aligned with your deeper calling.

The search for meaning often begins in moments of disruption: loss, illness, heartbreak, or the quiet realization that you are living someone else's dream instead of your own. These moments, though painful, are sacred. They crack you open and force you to ask, "What truly matters to me?"

Viktor Frankl, a Holocaust survivor and psychiatrist, observed that those who endured the camps often had a reason to live; a purpose that gave suffering meaning. He discovered that humans can endure almost anything when they have a why. Purpose is not a luxury. It is essential for resilience, survival, and growth.

Still, the search for meaning can be frustrating. We want a clear answer, a lightning bolt moment, a voice from the heavens declaring our purpose. Instead, purpose often reveals itself gradually, through patterns, whispers, synchronicities, and quiet nudges. It requires patience, awareness, and trust.

Sometimes the search leads us back to the things we loved as children, before the world told us who to be. Sometimes it leads us to our deepest wounds, which become sources of healing for others. Sometimes it leads us to quiet service, unseen by applause but deeply felt by those we touch.

The search itself is part of the purpose. The willingness to ask, to explore, and to remain open is sacred work. You are not lost. You are becoming. And every step of seeking brings you closer to the truth.

Discovering Your Unique Calling

Your purpose is not something outside of you waiting to be discovered. It is something within you waiting to be expressed. It lives at the intersection of your gifts, passions, values, and the world's needs. It is what energizes you, what makes you lose track of time, and what you would do even without recognition or reward.

Discovering your calling begins with attention. What energizes you? What stirs your anger? What fills you with joy? What injustice makes your heart ache? Purpose often lives where what you love meets what the world needs. It is where your deep gladness meets the world's deep hunger, as theologian Frederick Buechner wrote.

Your calling will not look like anyone else's, and that is the point. Comparison is the thief of purpose. Your experiences, skills, wounds, and insights are not random. They are preparing. Even your hardest chapters carry clues to what you are here to do.

Some people discover their purpose early and remain steady. Others wander for years before clarity emerges. Some live with one overarching purpose for a lifetime. Others move through seasons of purpose, each calling aligned with a different chapter. All of these paths are valid. Purpose does not need to be permanent to be meaningful.

Discovering your calling also requires releasing what is not yours to carry. Sometimes clarity comes not from deciding what to pursue, but from letting go of expectations, roles, and obligations that no longer fit. When you stop trying to be everything to everyone, you create space to become who you truly are.

Your purpose does not require permission or validation. It does not wait for perfect conditions. It begins the moment you say yes to it. It begins when you stop waiting to feel ready and start trusting that you are enough. Your calling is not something you earn. It is something you answer.

And here is the deeper truth: your purpose serves you as much as it serves others. When you live aligned with your calling, you feel alive, fulfilled, connected, and at peace. Purpose is not a sacrifice. It is an invitation to the life you were always meant to live.

Reflection: A Moment of Truth

I once worked with a woman named Maria who felt deeply lost. She had spent twenty years in a corporate career that paid well but left her empty. Every Sunday evening, she felt a knot in her stomach as she dreading Monday. She kept telling herself, "I should be grateful. People would kill for this job." But gratitude could not fill the void.

One day, during a difficult conversation with her teenage daughter, something shifted. Her daughter said, "Mom, you always tell me to follow my dreams. Why do you not follow yours?" The question hit like a lightning bolt. Maria realized she had been living on autopilot, following a script written by someone else.

She began asking herself uncomfortable questions: "If money were not an issue, what would I do? What did I love before I learned to ignore it? What breaks my heart in this world?" The answers surprised her. She had always been drawn to helping young women navigate difficult transitions, something she wished she had received in her own youth.

Maria did not quit her job overnight. Instead, she started small. She volunteered as a mentor. She took coaching classes. She began writing about her journey. Slowly, her purpose became clearer. Two years later, she transitioned into full-time work supporting young women through life transitions, including career changes, relationship challenges, and identity crises.

When I asked her what changed, she said, "I stopped waiting for permission. I stopped needing it to look a certain way. I started trusting that my story, my pain, my lessons, my growth, was exactly what someone else needed to hear. My purpose was not out there. It was in here all along."

Maria's income decreased initially, but her joy multiplied. She felt alive in a way she had not felt in decades. She realized that purpose is not about doing something impressive. It is about doing something true. And truth, when lived fully, is always enough.

Wisdom to Carry Forward

"The purpose of life is not to be happy. It is to be useful, to be honorable, to be compassionate, to have it make some difference that you have lived and lived well." (*Ralph Waldo Emerson*)

"Your purpose in life is to find your purpose and give your whole heart and soul to it." (*Buddha*)

"The meaning of life is to find your gift. The purpose of life is to give it away." (*Pablo Picasso*)

Affirmation

I trust my calling. I honor my gifts. My life has purpose, and I live it fully.

Journal Prompts

Take time to reflect deeply on these questions:

- What did I love doing as a child before the world told me who to be?
- What issue or injustice stirs my heart and makes me want to act?
- When do I feel most alive, most energized, most like myself?

- What would I do even if no one paid me, noticed me, or applauded me?
- If I knew I could not fail, what would I pursue?
- What experiences, even painful ones, have prepared me for something important?
- What do people consistently ask for my help with?

Soul Practice

The Purpose Discovery Map

This exercise helps you identify patterns and clues pointing toward your purpose.

1. Get a large piece of paper or a journal spread. Draw four overlapping circles labeled:

   - What I Love, passions, joys, interests
   - What I Am Good At, skills, talents, strengths
   - What the World Needs: problems that call to you, people who need help
   - What Brings Meaning, values, legacy, impact

1. Fill each circle with as many answers as you can. Do not filter or judge. Write everything.
2. Look at where the circles overlap. What shows up in multiple circles?
3. In the center, where all four circles meet, write potential expressions of your purpose.

4. Choose one small action you can take this week toward that purpose. Examples include:

- Research organizations doing this work
- Reach out to someone living this purpose
- Take a class or workshop
- Volunteer your time
- Start a project, even if it is small

5. Revisit this map quarterly. Purpose evolves as you do. What mattered last year may shift. Stay curious, not rigid.

Guided Meditation

Close your eyes. Take three deep breaths. Let your body relax completely.

Imagine yourself standing at the end of your life, looking back. You see the entire journey, the highs, the lows, the moments that mattered most.

From this perspective, ask yourself: "What am I most proud of? What brought me the deepest joy? What gave my life meaning?"

Allow the answers to arise without forcing them. Notice what your soul whispers from that future place of wisdom.

Now imagine your younger self, the child you were before the world told you who to be. See them clearly, full of dreams, wonder, and authenticity.

Ask them: "What did you come here to do? What was your greatest wish for this life?"

Listen. Receive their answer with love.

Now bring your awareness back to the present moment. You are here now, with time still ahead of you.

Whisper softly: "I am ready to live my purpose. I am ready to honor my calling. I am ready to become who I was meant to be."

Feel the energy of that commitment filling your body. Feel the truth of it resonating in your heart.

When you are ready, open your eyes. You know what to do. Your soul has been telling you all along.

Insight to Carry Forward

Purpose is not a destination. It is a direction. It is not something you achieve once and forget. It is something you live daily through choices, actions, and alignment. You do not need to have it all figured out. You only need to take the next step. Your purpose unfolds one choice at a time, one moment of courage at a time, one act of authenticity at a time. Trust the journey. The next chapter invites you to deepen the foundation that sustains purpose: cultivating self-love and embracing your inherent worthiness.

CHAPTER 17
Cultivating Self-Love and Worthiness
Why Self-Love Matters

Self-love is not vanity, indulgence, or narcissism. It is the radical act of believing you are worthy of kindness, respect, and care, simply because you exist. It is treating yourself with the same compassion you offer others. It is refusing to abandon yourself in pursuit of approval, achievement, or perfection.

When you love yourself, you do not wait to be "good enough" to deserve care. You do not postpone joy until you meet impossible standards. You do not punish yourself for being human. Instead, you honor your needs, celebrate your growth, and forgive your missteps. You become your own safe place.

Self-love matters because it is the foundation of everything else. Without it, every relationship becomes a search for validation. Every achievement becomes proof of worth. Every mistake becomes evidence of failure. With self-love, relationships become connections instead of transactions. Achievements become celebrations instead of requirements. Mistakes become teachers instead of verdicts.

Self-love is not something you achieve once and maintain forever. It is a daily practice, a conscious choice, and a commitment you renew again and again. Some days it feels natural. Other days, it feels impossible. Every time you choose yourself, your rest, your boundaries, and your truth, you strengthen the muscle of self-love.

The world will not always encourage self-love. You will be told to work harder, sacrifice more, and shrink smaller. You may be rewarded for selflessness and punished for self-care. Here is the truth: you cannot pour from an empty cup. You cannot love others well if you do not love yourself first. Self-love is not selfish. It is essential.

When you cultivate self-love, you stop seeking permission to exist fully. You stop apologizing for taking up space. You stop dimming your light to make others comfortable. You become unapologetically yourself, flawed, imperfect, worthy, and whole.

The Roots of Unworthiness

Unworthiness is learned. You were not born questioning your value. You were born knowing it. Somewhere along the way, the world taught you to doubt. Perhaps you were told you were too much or not enough. Perhaps love felt conditional and earned through performance rather than given freely. Perhaps you internalized messages that said your worth depended on what you did rather than who you were.

Unworthiness often begins in childhood. When caregivers are inconsistent, critical, or absent, children may internalize the belief that they are unlovable. When praise is tied to achievement, children learn that love is conditional. When mistakes are met with shame instead of guidance, children learn that imperfection is unacceptable.

Trauma deepens unworthiness. If you experienced abuse, neglect, or betrayal, you may have concluded that you deserved it. Trauma can convince people that what happened was their fault, that they are fundamentally flawed, or that they are not worthy of safety or love. These beliefs, though false, become deeply rooted.

Society reinforces unworthiness through impossible standards. We are told we are not thin enough, successful enough, attractive enough, productive enough, social enough, or wealthy enough. The goalpost constantly moves, ensuring we never feel adequate. This is by design.

Unworthiness sells products, feeds comparison, and keeps people small.

Unworthiness shows up in subtle ways. It is the voice that says, "Who do you think you are?" when you dream big. It is the hesitation before speaking up. It is the acceptance of disrespect because you believe you do not deserve better. It is the exhaustion that comes from constantly proving your value to others and to yourself.

Here is what you must know. Unworthiness is a lie. It is a story you were told, not a truth about who you are. Your worth is not earned. It is inherent. You are valuable not because of what you do, but because of what you are: a human being deserving of love, dignity, and belonging. You always have been. You always will be.

The Practice of Self-Love

Self-love is not a feeling you wait for. It is a practice you cultivate. It begins with small, consistent acts of kindness toward yourself. It is choosing rest when you are tired, even when productivity culture insists otherwise. It is nourishing your body with care rather than punishment. It is speaking to yourself with compassion instead of cruelty.

Self-love means honoring your needs without guilt. It means saying no to what depletes you and yes to what nourishes you. It means protecting your energy, your time, and your peace, not selfishly, but wisely. You cannot serve from depletion. You cannot give what you do not have.

Self-love also means accepting yourself as you are right now, not as you wish you were or hope to be someday. This does not mean you stop growing. It means you stop making growth a prerequisite for love. You are worthy now. Not when you lose weight, get the promotion, heal the wound, or fix the flaw. Now.

Forgiveness is a cornerstone of self-love. You will make mistakes. You will hurt people. You will fall short of your own expectations. Self-love means forgiving yourself with the same grace you offer others. It means understanding that mistakes do not define you. They refine you.

Self-love requires boundaries. It means protecting yourself from people, situations, and environments that diminish you. It means walking away from relationships that demand you shrink. It means refusing to tolerate disrespect, even from yourself. Boundaries are not walls. They are bridges to healthier connections.

Finally, self-love means celebrating yourself. Not just your achievements, but your existence. Your resilience. Your kindness. Your courage to keep going. You do not need to wait for someone else to see your value. You can see it. You can honor it. You can celebrate it today.

Self-love is one of the most revolutionary acts you can commit in a world that profits from self-doubt. When you love yourself, you disrupt systems built on unworthiness. You become free.

Reflection: A Moment of Truth

There was a time when I looked in the mirror and saw only flaws. Every wrinkle felt like a failure. Every extra pound seemed like evidence of inadequacy. I spoke to myself the way I would never speak to anyone else: harsh, critical, and unforgiving.

One morning, exhausted from the constant self-criticism, I asked myself a simple question: "What would happen if I spoke to myself the way I speak to my best friend?"

That question stopped me cold. I realized I would never tell my friend she was not good enough, not pretty enough, or not worthy enough. I would never shame her for being imperfect. Yet I did this to myself daily, believing that cruelty would somehow motivate me to become better.

So, I started an experiment. Every time I caught myself in negative self-talk, I paused and reframed it. "You are doing your best." "You are worthy of kindness." "You are allowed to rest." At first, the words felt false, as though I were lying to myself. But I kept going.

Slowly, something shifted. The harsh voice grew quieter. The kind voice grew louder. I began treating myself with the tenderness I had spent years giving to everyone else. I started honoring my needs, setting boundaries, and choosing rest without guilt.

Self-love did not happen overnight. It was a daily, imperfect, and ongoing practice. Over time, however, I noticed something profound. When I loved myself, I had more love to give. When I honored my worth, I stopped seeking validation. When I accepted myself, I stopped performing for approval.

Self-love was not selfish. It was liberating. And it changed everything.

Wisdom to Carry Forward

"You yourself, as much as anybody in the entire universe, deserve your love and affection."(*Buddha*)

"Loving yourself is not vanity. It is sanity." (*André Gide*)

"To fall in love with yourself is the first secret to happiness."(*Robert Morley)*

Affirmation

I am worthy of love, especially my own. I honor myself. I choose myself.

Journal Prompts

Take time to reflect deeply on these questions:

- How do I speak to myself when I make a mistake? Would I speak to a friend this way?
- What does self-love look like for me today?
- What needs have I been ignoring in the name of productivity or people pleasing?
- What would change if I truly believed I was worthy right now, exactly as I am?

- How can I celebrate myself today, not for what I did, but for who I am?
- What childhood messages about worthiness am I ready to release?

Soul Practice

The Self-Love Inventory

This practice helps you assess and strengthen your relationship with yourself.

1. Rate yourself on a scale of 1 to 10 in each area of self-love:

   - Self-Compassion: How kindly do I speak to myself?
   - Self-Care: How well do I honor my physical and emotional needs?
   - Self-Trust: How much do I trust my own judgment and intuition?
   - Self-Acceptance: How fully do I accept myself as I am right now?
   - Self-Forgiveness: How easily do I forgive myself for mistakes?
   - Self-Celebration: How often do I acknowledge my strengths and growth?

1. For any area rated below seven, ask:

   - What is blocking me from loving myself fully here?

- What one small action could I take this week to improve this area?

2. Choose one area to focus on this month. Write a commitment:

   "This month, I commit to strengthening my [self-compassion, self-care, etc.] by…"

3. Create daily reminders. Examples include:

   - A phone alarm with an affirmation
   - A mirror note with kind words
   - A calendar reminder to check in with yourself

4. At the end of the month, reassess your rating. Celebrate growth. Notice what shifts when you prioritize self-love.

Guided Meditation

Close your eyes. Place both hands over your heart. Feel its steady rhythm.

Take a deep breath and whisper, "I am here. I am worthy. I am loved."

Imagine a warm, golden light glowing in your chest. This light is pure love, unconditional, unwavering, and infinite.

Feel it spreading through your body, into your arms, your legs, and your head. Every cell is bathed in this loving light.

As it spreads, it dissolves criticism, shame, and doubt. It fills the spaces where unworthiness once lived with compassion, acceptance, and peace.

Whisper to yourself, "I forgive you. I accept you. I love you."

See yourself as a child, innocent, precious, and deserving. Wrap your arms around that child and say, "You are enough. You have always been enough."

Feel the truth of those words settling into your bones. You are not broken. You are not flawed. You are worthy, completely, entirely, and always.

Stay in this light as long as you need. When you are ready, open your eyes.

Carry this love with you. It is yours. It has always been yours. And no one, not even you, can take it away.

Insight to Carry Forward

Self-love is not the end of the journey. It is the beginning. When you love yourself, you create space for authentic connection, meaningful purpose, and deep peace. You stop living for approval and start living for alignment. You stop performing and start being. The next chapter invites you to extend that love outward by building a support system that honors and nurtures your wholeness.

CHAPTER 18
Building Your Support System Why Support Matters

You were never meant to do this alone. Healing, growing, and becoming are not solo journeys. They require witnesses, companions, and guides who walk beside you when the path feels dark. Support is not weakness. It is wisdom. It is the recognition that we are stronger together than we are apart.

A strong support system provides what you cannot always give yourself: perspective when you feel lost, encouragement when you doubt, accountability when you waver, and celebration when you succeed. It is the safety net that catches you when you fall and the lift that helps you rise higher.

Support matters because isolation breeds suffering. When we carry our pain alone, it grows heavier. When we hide our struggles, shame thrives. When we pretend to be fine, we disconnect from the very connection that could heal us. But when we let others in, when we share our truth, our fears, and our hopes, we discover we are not alone. That discovery changes everything.

The right support system does not fix you. It sees you. It does not solve your problems. It holds space for your process. It does not judge your struggles. It honors your humanity. True support says, "I see you. I believe in you. You are not too much, and you are not alone."

Support also provides accountability. When you share your goals, challenges, and commitments with trusted people, you are more likely to follow through. Not because they will punish you if you fail, but because they will remind you of your why when you forget. They reflect your strength back to you when you feel weak.

Building a support system is not about collecting as many people as possible. It is about cultivating a few authentic relationships where you can show up fully, messy, imperfect, and real. Quality over quantity. Depth over breadth. Connection over collection.

You deserve support. Not someday when you are "better," or "stronger," or "less needy." Now. Today. Exactly as you are. Asking for help is not a sign of failure. It is a sign of courage. It takes strength to admit you need someone, and wisdom to let them in.

The Cost of Isolation

Isolation is one of the heaviest weights a soul can carry. It whispers lies: "No one would understand." "I do not want to burden anyone." "I should be able to handle this myself." These lies keep you locked in loneliness, convinced that connection is unavailable or undeserved.

When we isolate, we rob ourselves of perspective. Our problems grow larger in the echo chamber of our own minds. Our fears become facts. Our worst-case scenarios become certainties. Without other voices to offer different viewpoints, we become trapped in our own narratives, often the most critical and hopeless ones.

Isolation also drains energy. Pretending to be okay when you are not is exhausting. Hiding your struggles takes more energy than sharing them. The mask of being "fine" is heavy, and wearing it constantly leaves you depleted, disconnected, and discouraged.

Research confirms what the heart already knows. Chronic isolation increases the risk of depression, anxiety, and even physical illness. Loneliness affects the body in ways similar to chronic stress, raising inflammation, weakening immunity, and shortening lifespan. We are wired for connection. Without it, we wither.

Perhaps the deepest cost of isolation is this: you never get to experience being fully known and still fully loved. You never discover that your imperfections do not disqualify you from belonging. You never learn that vulnerability is not rejection. It is an invitation.

Isolation convinces you that you are the only one struggling, the only one who feels this way, the only one who has not figured it out. The truth is that everyone is fighting battles you cannot see. Everyone carries wounds they have not shared. When you break the silence and reach out, you often discover the simple truth: "Me too. I thought I was the only one."

That moment when isolation dissolves, and connection begins, is sacred. It reminds you that you are not alone. You never were. You simply needed to reach out.

Cultivating Authentic Connection

Not all relationships are created equal. Some people drain you, while others nourish you. Some relationships are transactional, while others are transformational. Building a support system means being intentional about who you allow into your inner circle and what role they play in your life.

An authentic connection requires vulnerability. It means showing up as you are, not as you think you should be. It means sharing your truth, even when it feels risky. It means letting people see your struggles, not just your successes. Vulnerability is the bridge to intimacy. Without it, relationships remain surface-level.

Look for people who celebrate your growth, not just your achievements. People who ask how you are and wait for the real answer. People who do not try to fix you, but who are willing to sit with you in the mess. People who reflect your worth to you when you forget it.

Healthy support includes different types of relationships, each serving a unique purpose. Some people are your cheerleaders. They believe in you fiercely and remind you of your potential. Some are your truth tellers. They love you enough to call you out when you are not living aligned. Some are your safe spaces. They hold your pain without judgment. Some are your mirrors. They reflect patterns you cannot see on your own.

Building support also requires reciprocity. Healthy relationships are not one-sided. You must be willing to give as well as receive, to show up for others as they show up for you. This is not about keeping score. It is about mutual care, respect, and investment.

Not everyone from your past belongs in your future. As you grow and change, some relationships will naturally shift or end. This is not failure. It is evolution. Honor what was, but do not cling to relationships that no longer serve your highest good. It is okay to outgrow people. It is okay to choose yourself.

Cultivating connection also means seeking professional support when needed. Therapists, coaches, counselors, and support groups are not signs of weakness. They are investments in your well-being. Sometimes the support you need most comes from someone trained to guide you through the depths.

Finally, remember that building a support system takes time. Trust is earned slowly through consistency and care. Do not rush intimacy. Start small. Share a little and notice how it is received. Let trust deepen gradually. The right people will prove themselves worthy of your openness.

Reflection: A Moment of Truth

For years, I prided myself on being independent. I told myself I didn't need anyone, that asking for help was a weakness. Beneath that pride was fear; fear of being a burden, fear of rejection, fear of being seen as incapable.

Then came a season when life became too heavy to carry alone. A personal loss shattered me, and for the first time, I could not pretend to be fine. I could not keep the mask on. I was drowning, and I knew it.

One evening, I sat across from a friend and said the hardest words I had ever spoken: "I am not okay. I need help." I expected judgment. I expected them to pull away. Instead, they leaned in.

"Thank you for trusting me with this," they said. "You are not alone. I am here."

Those words broke something open in me. I realized that my independence had been isolation disguised as strength. I had been so afraid of burdening others that I had denied them the gift of supporting me. I had forgotten that connection is not about perfection. It is about presence.

I began slowly opening up to a few trusted people. I joined a support group. I started therapy. I learned to ask for help without apologizing. Something miraculous happened: the more I let people in, the lighter I felt. The more I shared my struggles, the less power they had over me.

I also discovered something unexpected. My vulnerability permitted others to be vulnerable too. When I stopped pretending to have it all together, the people around me stopped pretending too. Real connection blossomed where performance had once lived.

Building a support system did not make me weak. It made me whole. I am still independent, but I am no longer isolated. I am still strong, but I am no longer alone. That has made all the difference.

Wisdom to Carry Forward

"We cannot walk alone." (*Martin Luther King Jr.*)

"Connection is why we are here. It is what gives purpose and meaning to our lives." (*Brené Brown*)

"The friend who can be silent with us in a moment of despair or confusion, who can stay with us in an hour of grief and bereavement, who can tolerate not knowing… that is a friend who cares." (*Henri Nouwen*)

Affirmation

I am worthy of support. I allow others to walk with me. I am not alone.

Journal Prompts

Take time to reflect deeply on these questions:

- Who are the people in my life who truly see me and accept me?
- Where have I been isolating instead of reaching out?
- What makes it hard for me to ask for help? What old belief is blocking me?
- What kind of support do I need most right now, and who could provide it?
- How can I be a better support to others in my life?
- What relationships do I need to release, and what new connections do I need to cultivate?

Soul Practice

The Support System Mapping Exercise

This practice helps you assess your current support and identify where to strengthen it.

1. Draw three concentric circles on a page:

   - Inner Circle: Your closest, most trusted relationships (2–5 people)
   - Middle Circle: Important but less intimate connections (5–10 people)
   - Outer Circle: Acquaintances and casual connections

2. Write names in each circle. For each person in your Inner and Middle Circles, note:

   - What they provide (emotional support, practical help, accountability, fun, wisdom)
   - How often do you connect?
   - Whether the relationship feels balanced

1. Reflect:

   - Is my Inner Circle truly supportive, or are there people who drain me?
   - Are there gaps? Do I need more emotional support, accountability, or joy?
   - Who could move from the Middle to the Inner Circle with more investment?
   - Are there toxic relationships I need to move outward or release entirely?

2. Identify 1–3 action steps:

   - "I will reach out to [person] this week and share something real."

- "I will join [support group/class/community] to meet like-minded people."
- "I will create distance from [person/situation] that consistently drains me."

3. Remember: Quality over quantity. A few deep connections matter more than many shallow ones.

Guided Meditation

Close your eyes. Take a deep breath. Feel your body grounding.

Imagine standing in a circle of light. This light represents love, support, and connection.

Now, one by one, invite into this circle the people who have supported you, past and present. See their faces. Feel their presence.

Whisper to each one, "Thank you for seeing me. Thank you for walking with me."

Feel the warmth of their love surrounding you. You are not alone. You never were.

Now imagine inviting your future self into the circle, the version of you who has found even deeper connection, who has let even more people in.

Ask them, "What do you want me to know about support?"

Listen. Receive their wisdom.

Place your hand on your heart and repeat, "I am worthy of support. I am allowed to need people. Connection is my birthright."

When ready, open your eyes. Carry this knowing with you. You belong. You are held. You are never alone.

Insight to Carry Forward

Building a support system is not a one-time task. It is an ongoing practice of tending to relationships, asking for help, and allowing yourself to be seen. The people who walk with you on this journey matter as much as the journey itself. You do not have to be strong alone. You were never meant to be. The next chapter invites you to integrate everything you have learned; to live awake, whole, and fully embodied in your truth.

CHAPTER 19
Living Awake and Whole What It Means to Be Awake

To live awake is to live with eyes wide open to the truth of who you are, to the patterns that no longer serve you, to the beauty and pain of being human. It is to stop sleepwalking through your days and start showing up fully, consciously, and intentionally. Awakeness is not a destination you reach; it is a practice you choose, again and again.

When you are awake, you notice. You notice when you are operating from fear instead of love. You notice when you are dimming your light to make others comfortable. You notice when you are betraying yourself to keep the peace. And in that noticing, you have the power to choose differently.

Being awake means living in alignment. Your actions match your values. Your words reflect your truth. Your choices honor your needs. There is no longer a gap between who you are and who you pretend to be. You stop performing and start being.

Awakeness also means accepting reality as it is, not as you wish it were. It means letting go of the exhausting fight against what is and embracing what can be changed. It is the serenity prayer embodied: changing what you can, accepting what you cannot, and knowing the difference.

To be awake is to feel everything: the joy and the grief, the hope and the fear, the gratitude and the anger. You do not numb, avoid, or suppress. You meet each emotion with presence and compassion. You understand that feeling is not weakness; it is aliveness.

Living awake means you stop waiting. You stop waiting for permission, for perfection, for the right time. You understand that life is happening now, and now is all you have. You stop postponing joy and start claiming it. You stop rehearsing for a life you will live someday and start living the life you have today.

Awakeness is both a gift and a responsibility. Once you see, you cannot unsee. Once you know, you cannot unknow. With that knowing comes the invitation and the obligation to live differently, to live true, to live whole.

The Practice of Wholeness

Wholeness is not the absence of brokenness; it is the integration of all your parts. It is making peace with your past, honoring your present, and trusting your future. It is gathering the scattered pieces of your soul and weaving them into something beautiful and complete.

To live whole means embracing your contradictions. You are strong and vulnerable, confident and uncertain, healed and healing. You contain multitudes, and that is not confusion; it is wholeness. You do not need to choose one side of yourself and abandon the other. You can hold it all.

Wholeness requires integration of everything this book has taught you: the awareness from Part One, the release from Part Two, the cultivation from Part Three, the embodiment from Part Four. These are not separate lessons; they are threads woven together to create the tapestry of your transformed life.

Living whole means you no longer fragment yourself to fit different spaces. You do not have a work self, a home self, and a friend self. You are simply you; consistent, authentic, integrated. What you believe privately, you express publicly. What you value internally, you demonstrate externally.

Wholeness also means honoring the sacred masculine and sacred feminine within you, regardless of your gender. The masculine: structure, action, direction, boundaries. The feminine: intuition, flow, receptivity, nurturing. Both are essential. Both are powerful. Wholeness is the marriage of both.

To practice wholeness is to commit to ongoing growth without making growth a requirement for love. You are whole now, and you are still becoming. You are complete as you are, and you are still evolving. These truths coexist. You do not need to be perfect to be whole; you just need to be willing.

Wholeness is not static; it is dynamic. It shifts as you shift, grows as you grow, deepens as you deepen. It is not something you achieve once and maintain forever. It is something you return to again and again, every time you lose your way and find yourself.

Daily Practices for Integration

Living awake and whole is not a philosophy; it is a practice. It is the accumulation of small, daily choices that honor your truth and nurture your soul. Integration does not happen by accident; it happens through intention, consistency, and commitment.

Start each day with intention. Before you check your phone, before you rush into doing, pause. Ask yourself: "How do I want to feel today? What matters most to me today? How can I honor myself today?" This simple morning practice sets the tone for everything that follows.

Throughout the day, practice presence. When you eat, eat. When you work, work. When you rest, rest. Stop multitasking your way through life. Give your full attention to the moment you are in. Presence is the antidote to the scattered, distracted existence that leaves you feeling empty.

Check in with yourself regularly. Set reminders throughout the day to pause and ask: "How am I feeling right now? What do I need? Am I aligned with my values in this moment?" This practice of checking in prevents you from drifting away from yourself.

Honor your emotional experience. When difficult emotions arise, do not push them away. Pause. Breathe. Name what you feel: "I am feeling anxious. I am feeling sad. I am feeling overwhelmed." Naming creates space. Space creates choice. Choice creates freedom.

Practice gratitude daily, not as toxic positivity that ignores pain, but as a lens that helps you see beauty alongside struggle. What brought you joy today? What are you grateful for? Who showed you kindness? Gratitude shifts your focus from scarcity to abundance.

Move your body with intention. Whether it is yoga, walking, dancing, or simply stretching, or moving. Your body holds wisdom. Your body carries stress. Movement releases, grounds, and reconnects you to yourself.

End each day with reflection. What went well? What challenged you? What did you learn? What will you do differently tomorrow? Reflection transforms experience into wisdom. Without it, you repeat patterns without learning from them.

Finally, be gentle with yourself. Some days you will embody these practices beautifully. Other days, you will forget them entirely. Both are okay. Integration is not perfection; it is progress. It is showing up, stumbling, rising, and trying again. That is wholeness. That is being human. That is enough.

Reflection: A Moment of Truth

I remember the moment I realized I was finally living awake. It was not dramatic or profound; it was ordinary. I was washing dishes, sunlight streaming through the window, warm water on my hands. And I felt present— fully there. Not thinking about yesterday or planning tomorrow, just there in that simple moment, feeling alive.

For years, I had chased awakening like it was some grand enlightenment, a lightning bolt moment that would change everything forever. But awakening was not an event. It was a thousand small choices. It was noticeable when I was people-pleasing and choosing authenticity instead. It was feeling my feelings instead of numbing them. It was saying no without guilt and yes with joy.

Wholeness came even more gradually. For so long, I believed I needed to fix all my broken pieces before I could be whole. But wholeness was not about erasing my scars; it was about integrating them. My wounds were not separate from my strength; they were part of it. My past was not something to overcome; it was something to honor as part of my story.

Living awake and whole does not mean I never struggle. I still have hard days. I still doubt myself sometimes. I still make mistakes. But now, I meet those moments differently. I do not spiral into shame. I do not abandon myself. I stay present. I extend compassion. I trust that I will figure it out.

The practices in this book, the meditations, the journal prompts, the soul work, are not things I did once and moved on from. They are companions I return to again and again. Some days I need the forgiveness practice. On other days, I need the boundary work. Each practice is a tool I can reach for when I need it.

Living awake and whole is not a destination I reached; it is a way of traveling. It is how I move through my days now—with more presence, more compassion, more authenticity, more peace. And on the days when I forget, when I slip back into old patterns, I have the tools to come home to myself again.

That is what this journey has given me: not perfection, but presence; not fixing, but wholeness; not arrival but awakening. And it is more than enough.

Wisdom to Carry Forward

"The privilege of a lifetime is to become who you truly are." (*Carl Jung*)

"Wholeness is not achieved by cutting off a portion of one's being, but by integration of the contraries." (*Carl Jung*)

"The soul always knows what to do to heal itself. The challenge is to silence the mind." (*Caroline Myss)*

Affirmation

I am awake. I am whole. I am living my truth fully and completely.

Journal Prompts

Take time to reflect deeply on these questions:

- In what areas of my life am I most awake? Where am I still sleepwalking?
- What does wholeness feel like in my body?
- Which practices from this book have served me most?

- How has my relationship with myself changed since beginning this journey?
- What do I want to integrate most deeply moving forward?
- How will I know I am living aligned with my truth?
- What support do I need to maintain this awakeness?

Soul Practice: The Integration Ritual

This practice helps you consolidate your learning and commit to ongoing growth.

1. Review Your Journey:

   - Flip through your journal entries from throughout this book
   - Notice patterns, growth, and shifts
   - Acknowledge how far you have come

Identify Your Core Practices:

   - Which 3-5 practices from this book feel most essential to your continued wholeness?
   - Write them down
   - Commit to incorporating them into your daily or weekly rhythm

1. Create Your Personal Integration Plan:

   - **Morning Practice (5-10 minutes):** Meditation, intention-setting, affirmation

- **Throughout the Day (Check-ins):** Hourly pause to breathe and assess alignment
- **Evening Practice (10-15 minutes):** Gratitude journaling, reflection, releasing the day
- **Weekly Practice (30-60 minutes):** Deeper journaling, soul practice exercise, meditation

2. Write a Letter to Your Future Self:

- What do you want to remember?
- What commitments are you making?
- What does living awake and whole mean to you?
- Read this letter monthly as a reminder

3. Create Accountability:

- Share your integration plan with someone you trust
- Schedule regular check-ins with yourself (calendar reminders)
- Consider finding an accountability partner or joining a community

4. Celebrate:

- Honor how far you have come
- Acknowledge your courage in doing this work
- Celebrate your commitment to living awake

Guided Meditation

Close your eyes. Take a deep breath. Feel your entire body from the crown of your head to the soles of your feet.

Imagine a warm, golden light beginning at your heart center. This light represents your wholeness, the integration of all you are and all you have learned.

With each breath, feel this light expanding, filling your chest, arms, legs, and entire being. It reaches into every corner, every cell, illuminating everything.

This light integrates your past and present, your wounds and wisdom, your pain and purpose. Everything belongs. Nothing is separate.

Whisper softly: "I am whole. I am integrated. I am awake."

See yourself moving through your days with this light glowing from within. You are present. You are authentic. You are aligned.

When challenges arise, this light remains. When doubt creeps in, this light holds steady. When you forget, this light reminds you: you are whole.

Place both hands over your heart and feel the warmth of your own wholeness. You are no longer fragmented. You are no longer lost. You are here, fully, completely.

Repeat: "I live awake. I live whole. I live true."

When you are ready, open your eyes. Carry this light with you. It is not something you must achieve; it is something you already are.

You are whole. You have always been whole. Welcome home.

Insight to Carry Forward

Living awake and whole is not the end of your journey; it is the beginning of living it fully. Every practice you have learned, every insight you have gained, every pattern you have broken, these are not steps to complete and forget. They are tools to carry with you, companions to return to, anchors to ground you when life gets stormy. You are not finished. You will never be finished. And that is the point. Growth is not a destination; it is a way of being. Wholeness is not static; it is alive. And you, dear soul, are more awake than you have ever been. The final chapter invites you to step forward with this awakened awareness and continue the journey that never truly ends.

CHAPTER 20
The Journey Continues You Are Not the Same

If you have traveled this far, you are not the same person who opened this book. Something has shifted. Something has awakened. Something has been remembered. You may not feel transformed every moment, and transformation is not linear, but you are different. You know things now that you cannot unknow. You see things now that you cannot unsee.

You understand that you are not broken. You never were. You were simply disconnected from yourself, from your truth, from your wholeness. But through the pages of this book, through the practices and reflections, you have been finding your way home.

You have learned to recognize the patterns that kept you stuck and chosen new ones. You have met your emotions with compassion instead of fear. You have reclaimed your authentic self and healed your inner child. You have practiced forgiveness, embraced vulnerability, and discovered the power of presence. You have cultivated gratitude, welcomed change, and learned to live with intention.

You have released what no longer serves you, including resentment, perfectionism, and control. You have built practices that nourish your soul, foster self-compassion, cultivate surrender, establish boundaries, and build self-trust. You have awakened to your purpose, embraced your worthiness, and built a support system that honors your journey.

And now you know: healing is not a destination. Growth is not a finish line. Wholeness is not something you achieve once and maintain forever. It is something you return to, again and again, with each choice, each breath, each moment of presence.

You are different now because you have done the work. You have shown up for yourself. You have chosen courage over comfort, truth over performance, authenticity over approval. And that willingness, the commitment to the hard, sacred work of becoming, has changed everything.

The Path Ahead

This book may be ending, but your journey is not. In fact, it is just beginning. Everything you have learned here is not meant to be read once and forgotten; it is meant to be lived, practiced, and embodied. These chapters are not steps to complete; they are companions to return to whenever you need them.

There will be days when you forget everything you have learned. Days when old patterns resurface; days when you feel lost again. This is not failure; it is being human. Growth is not linear, and healing spirals. You will revisit the same lessons at deeper levels, again and again, and that is okay. That is the journey.

When you forget, come back to the practices. Return to the meditations. Reread the chapters that speak to where you are now. This book is not a manual you outgrow; it is a companion you carry with you. Let it be a touchstone, a reminder, a map when the path feels unclear.

The path ahead will not always be easy. There will be challenges you did not anticipate, losses you did not see coming, transitions that shake your foundation. But now you have tools. You have practices. You have a framework for navigating the unknown. You know how to meet yourself with compassion. You know how to ask for support. You know how to trust yourself, even when the path forward is uncertain.

The path ahead will also be beautiful. There will be moments of profound joy, unexpected grace, and deep peace. There will be connections that nourish your soul, work that lights you up, and days when you feel so alive you could burst. And when those moments come, you will be present for them. You will not rush past them. You will savor them. Because now you know how.

The journey continues, and you are ready for it. Not because you have all the answers, but because you are willing to keep asking the questions. Not because you are perfect, but because you are committed to showing up imperfectly. Not because you have arrived, but because you trust the process of becoming.

Walk forward with courage. Walk forward with compassion. Walk forward with the knowing that you are exactly where you need to be.

As you close this book and step back into your life, know this: you are not alone. You have never been alone. Every soul who has walked this path of awakening has felt what you feel: the doubt, the fear, the uncertainty, and the hope.

There is a community of seekers, healers, and warriors walking alongside you, some you have met, others you have not yet encountered. They are on their own journeys, doing their own work, asking their own questions. And though your paths may differ, your hearts beat with the same truth: we are worthy, we are whole, we are becoming.

When the journey feels heavy, reach out. Share your truth. Ask for support. Let others walk with you. You do not have to carry this alone. In fact, you were never meant to. Connection is not a luxury. It is essential. We heal in community. We grow in relationships. We thrive in belonging.

Remember, too, that you are not alone in your struggles. Everyone, everyone, is navigating their own pain, their own patterns, their own path to wholeness. The difference is not that some people have it all figured out. The difference is that some people have learned to meet themselves with compassion. And now, you are one of them.

You are also not alone because the wisdom you carry is ancient. You are part of a lineage of seekers who have asked these questions before you. The practices in this book, meditation, reflection, presence, and compassion, have been guiding souls home for centuries. You are connected to something far larger than yourself.

And finally, you are not alone because your soul has been with you all along. Through every dark night, every wrong turn, every moment you felt lost, your soul was there, whispering, guiding, waiting for you to listen. That whisper brought you to this book. That whisper will continue to guide you forward.

You are held. You are supported. You are loved. Always.

Reflection: A Moment of Truth

I want to share something with you before we part ways. This book, the words you have read, the practices you have tried, the truths you have uncovered, did not come from some enlightened place where I have all the answers. It came from the trenches, from my own journey through pain, confusion, healing, and awakening.

I wrote this book because I needed it. I needed someone to tell me I was not broken. I needed someone to hold my hand through the darkness and remind me that wholeness was possible. I needed practices that were not just theoretical, but practical, not just inspiring, but actionable. And when I could not find that book, I decided to write it.

But here is what I know now: I was not writing this book for me. I was writing it for you. Your soul whispered you here because you needed these words, these practices, this reminder. And my soul whispered to me here to deliver them.

This is not goodbye. This is an invitation. An invitation to continue the journey, not alone, but together. Through *The Soul's Experience*, I walk alongside people just like you, people who are ready to remember their wholeness, reclaim their truth, and live their purpose.

If this book has resonated with you, if you feel called to go deeper, if you want support as you integrate these practices into your daily life, I am here. I would be honored to walk with you. Not as someone who has all the answers, but as someone who is willing to sit with the questions alongside you.

Because here is the truth: we are all walking each other home. And the path is less lonely when we walk it together.

Thank you for trusting me with your journey. Thank you for doing this work. Thank you for choosing yourself. The world needs your light, not someday when you are healed enough, but now. Today. Exactly as you are.

Your soul whispered you here for a reason. Trust that whisper. Follow where it leads. And know that I am cheering for you every step of the way.

Wisdom to Carry Forward

"The journey of a thousand miles begins with one step." (*Lao Tzu*)

"We are not human beings having a spiritual experience. We are spiritual beings having a human experience." (*Pierre Teilhard de Chardin*)

"And the day came when the risk to remain tight in a bud was more painful than the risk it took to blossom." (*Anaïs Nin*)

Affirmation

I am ready. I am worthy. I am becoming. The journey continues, and I walk it with courage.

Journal Prompts

Take time to reflect deeply on these questions:

- How am I different now than when I started this book?
- What is the most important lesson I have learned?
- Which practice will I commit to continuing daily?
- What support do I need as I move forward?
- What does living my truth look like in practical terms?
- How will I celebrate how far I have come?
- What is my soul whispering to me now?

Soul Practice

Your Commitment Ceremony

This final practice honors your journey and invites you to commit to the path ahead.

1. Find a quiet, sacred space. Light a candle if you wish.
2. Reflect on Your Journey:

- Where were you when you started this book?
- What have you learned?
- How have you grown?

Write it down. Acknowledge it. Celebrate it.

1. Release What No Longer Serves:

   - Write down any beliefs, patterns, or identities you are releasing.
   - Speak them aloud: "I release…"
   - Tear or burn the paper safely as a symbol of letting go.

1. Claim Your Truth:

   - Write a declaration of who you are now and who you are becoming.
   - Begin with: "I am…"
   - Examples: "I am worthy. I am whole. I am brave. I am becoming."
   - Speak this declaration aloud with conviction.

2. Make Your Commitment:

   - What practices will you continue?
   - What support will you seek?
   - What does living your truth look like moving forward?
   - Write this as a commitment to yourself.

3. Seal Your Intention:

    - Place your hand on your heart.
    - Take three deep breaths.
    - Say: "I commit to honoring myself. I commit to my wholeness. I commit to the journey."

4. Keep your declaration somewhere visible. Return to it whenever you need to remember.

Guided Meditation

Close your eyes one final time. Take a deep, nourishing breath.

Imagine yourself standing at a crossroads. Behind you is the path you have traveled, every step, every struggle, every breakthrough. See how far you have come. Honor that journey.

Ahead of you stretches a path illuminated by golden light. This is your future, unknown, unwritten, and full of possibilities.

Feel the wisdom you carry in your bones. Feel the practices you have learned living in your body. Feel the truth you have reclaimed pulsing in your heart.

You are not the same. You are awake. You are whole. You are ready.

Whisper to yourself: "I trust the journey. I trust myself. I am exactly where I need to be."

See yourself stepping forward onto that illuminated path. With each step, you carry everything you have learned. With each step, you honor who you are becoming.

You are not walking alone. Around you are souls, seen and unseen, walking their own paths and carrying their own light. You are part of something vast, ancient, and beautiful.

Place both hands over your heart and feel its steady beat. This is your compass. This is your truth. This will always guide you home.

Take one more deep breath. When you open your eyes, know this: the journey continues, and you are ready.

Open your eyes. Welcome home to yourself.

A Final Word

This is not the end. This is a beginning. You have been given tools, practices, and truths that will serve you for the rest of your life. Return to them often. Share them generously. Live them fully. Your soul whispered to you to be here because you needed this. Now, your soul is calling you forward to live your truth, honor your wholeness, and become who you were always meant to be. The journey continues, and I am deeply grateful that you are walking it. With deep love and unwavering belief in you. - Beronica

RESOURCES FOR YOUR JOURNEY Daily Soul Practice Toolkit

This toolkit provides daily practices to support your journey back to yourself. Use these tools as needed and adapt them to your unique path.

Morning Ritual

1. Upon waking, place your hand on your heart and take three deep breaths.
2. Set an intention for the day: "Today, I choose…"
3. Write three things you are grateful for.
4. Read your daily affirmation.
5. Spend five minutes in silent meditation or journaling.

Evening Reflection

1. Review your day without judgment.
2. Journal: "What did I learn about myself today?"
3. Acknowledge one moment you showed up authentically.
4. Release what you cannot control.
5. End with a gratitude prayer or meditation.

Weekly Practices

- **Soul Sunday:** Spend 30 minutes in nature, silence, or creative expression.

- **Midweek Check-in:** Review your journal prompts and track your growth.
- **Boundary Review:** Assess where you need to strengthen or soften boundaries.
- **Self-Care Ritual:** Schedule something that nourishes your soul.

30-DAY INTEGRATION GUIDE

This guide helps you integrate the teachings from this book into your daily life. Each week builds upon the last.

Week 1: Awareness

- Days 1–2: Complete Chapter 1 exercises.
- Days 3–4: Journal on patterns you notice.
- Days 5–6: Practice The Whisper Exercise daily.
- Day 7: Rest and reflect.

Week 2: Release

- Days 8–9: Work through Chapter 2 Pattern Mapping.
- Days 10–11: Identify one pattern to release.
- Days 12–13: Practice choosing differently.
- Day 14: Celebrate your courage.

Week 3: Feel

- Days 15–16: Chapter 3 Emotional Check-Ins.
- Days 17–18: Allow yourself to feel without judgment.
- Days 19–20: Practice compassionate self-talk.
- Day 21: Honor your emotional journey.

Week 4: Integrate & Continue

- Days 22–24: Review your journal from Weeks 1–3.

- Days 25–27: Create your personal Soul Practice.
- Days 28–29: Share your journey with a trusted person.
- Day 30: Commit to ongoing growth.

RECOMMENDED READING & RESOURCES

These books and resources complement the journey you have begun:

On Healing and Wholeness

- *The Body Keeps the Score* by Bessel van der Kolk, M.D.
- *What Happened to You?* by Bruce D. Perry, M.D., Ph.D., and Oprah Winfrey
- The Gifts of Imperfection by Brené Brown, Ph.D.
- When Things Fall Apart by Pema Chödrön
- The Places That Scare You by Pema Chödrön

On Self-Compassion and Inner Work

- *Self-Compassion* by Kristin Neff, Ph.D.
- *Radical Acceptance* by Tara Brach, Ph.D.
- *The Power of Now* by Eckhart Tolle
- *Homecoming* by John Bradshaw
- It Didn't Start with You by Mark Wolynn

On Purpose and Authenticity

- *The Alchemist* by Paulo Coelho
- *Big Magic* by Elizabeth Gilbert
- *The Untethered Soul* by Michael A. Singer
- *A Return to Love* by Marianne Williamson

- *The Four Agreements* by Don Miguel Ruiz

Additional Resources

- The Soul's Experience website:

https://thesoulsexperience.com

- Trauma-informed therapists: Psychology Today therapist finder
- Guided meditations: Insight Timer, Calm, Headspace
- Journaling apps: Day One, Journey, Penzu

ABOUT THE SOUL'S EXPERIENCE

The Soul's Experience is a compassionate coaching practice dedicated to helping individuals reconnect with their authentic selves, heal from past wounds, and discover their life purpose.

Founded on the belief that you are not broken, only disconnected from your truth, our approach combines trauma-informed practices, emotional intelligence, and life purpose coaching to support your journey home to yourself.

Through one-on-one coaching, we create safe spaces for healing, growth, and awakening. Our work is rooted in the understanding that true transformation happens not through fixing, but through remembering who you have always been.

If this book has resonated with you and you would like support on your journey, we would be honored to walk alongside you.

For more information about our coaching programs and resources, please visit our website or reach out directly.

Remember: You are whole. You are worthy. You are home.

Connect with us:

- Website: https://thesoulsexperience.com
- Email: info@thesoulsexperience.com

May your soul continue to whisper, and may you always have the courage to listen.

ABOUT THE AUTHOR

Beronica Parham

(Founder of The Soul's Experience)

Beronica Parham knows what it feels like to carry pain that no one else can see. She knows the weight of indecision, the ache of feeling lost, and the courage it takes to whisper, "I need help." She has lived it. She has walked through the darkness, stumbled through the questions, and emerged, not unscathed, but transformed.

And now, she walks alongside others on their journey home to themselves.

As the founder of The Soul's Experience, Beronica has dedicated her life to a singular, powerful mission: helping people who are still carrying the invisible weight of trauma, pain, and indecision to rediscover their wholeness. Not by fixing them, because they were never broken, but by reminding them of the truth they have forgotten: You are worthy. You are enough. You are already home.

Beronica's approach is different because her story is different. This is not theory learned from textbooks or wisdom borrowed from others. This is lived experience. This is a hard-won truth. This is the kind of knowing that only comes from walking through your own fire and choosing to transform the ashes into light.

Her journey began in the same place many of her clients find themselves now, feeling disconnected, uncertain, and quietly wondering if wholeness was ever meant for them. Through her own healing process, Beronica discovered something profound: healing is not about becoming someone new. It is about remembering who you have always been beneath the layers of conditioning, trauma, and fear.

That discovery changed everything, and it became her calling.

Today, as a trauma-informed emotional intelligence and life purpose coach, Beronica creates sacred spaces where people feel safe to remove their masks, honor their pain, and reclaim their truth. Her work is rooted in compassion, informed by science, and guided by an unwavering belief in the resilience of the human spirit.

But what truly sets Beronica apart is not just her training or expertise; it is her heart. It is the way she sees people, not for their problems, but for their potential. It is the way she holds space for grief and joy, struggle and strength, questions and certainty. It is the way she reminds you, with every conversation, every exercise, every gentle challenge: You are not alone. You are not beyond help. You are not too broken to heal.

Because she has been there, she has felt that despair. And she has also felt the sun break through.

Beronica's work is not just about helping people survive; it is about helping them thrive. It is about guiding them from merely existing to fully living, from feeling stuck to feeling free, from questioning their worth to knowing it in their bones.

Through The Soul's Experience, Beronica offers one-on-one coaching, transformative workshops, and soul-centered programs that combine trauma-informed practices with emotional intelligence and life purpose discovery. Her approach is holistic, honoring the complexity of human experience while providing practical tools for real, lasting change.

She does not promise quick fixes or empty platitudes. She promises presence. She promises truth. She promises that if you are willing to do the work, she will walk every step with you, not ahead of you, not behind you, but beside you.

Because healing is not a solo journey, and neither is becoming.

Beronica continues her own journey of growth and healing, understanding that transformation is not a destination but a lifelong practice. She has her own support system, her own guides, her own moments of doubt and breakthrough. And that is what makes her work so powerful; she is not teaching from a pedestal; she is sharing from the path.

This book, *This Book Found You Because Your Soul Whispered*, is the culmination of everything Beronica has learned, lived, and longed to share. It is her love letter to anyone who has ever felt lost. It is her map for anyone seeking their way home. She promises that wholeness is not only possible, but it is your birthright.

If you are reading this, it is no accident. Your soul called you here. And Beronica is honored to be part of your journey.

Because she knows something essential: The world needs your light. Not someday, when you are "healed enough" or "ready enough." Now. Today. Exactly as you are.

You are not broken. You are becoming.

And Beronica is here to remind you of that truth, again and again, for as long as you need to hear it.

Work with Beronica

If this book has resonated with you and you are ready to take the next step on your journey, Beronica would be honored to support you.

Through The Soul's Experience, she offers:

- 30 min Healing Isn't Linear Support & Strategy Session
- One-on-One Coaching: Personalized guidance for your unique healing journey

Connect with Beronica and The Soul's Experience:

- Website: https://thesoulsexperience.com
- Email: info@thesoulsexperience.com
- Instagram: @thesoulsexperience

"Your soul whispered you here. Now let it guide you home."

Beronica Parham